The History and Impact of Marxist-Leninist Organizational Theory:

"Useful Idiots," "Innocents' Clubs," and "Transmission Belts"

John P. Roche

Foreign Policy Report
April 1984

INSTITUTE FOR FOREIGN POLICY ANALYSIS, INC.
Cambridge, Massachusetts, and Washington, D.C.

Requests for copies of IFPA Foreign Policy Reports should be addressed to the Circulation Manager, Foreign Policy Reports, Institute for Foreign Policy Analysis, Inc., Central Plaza Building, Tenth Floor, 675 Massachusetts Avenue, Cambridge, Massachusetts 02139. (Telephone: 617-492-2116) Please send a check or money order for the correct amount along with your order.

Standing orders for all Foreign Policy Reports will be accepted by the Circulation Manager. Standing order subscribers will automatically receive all future Reports as soon as they are published. Each Report will be accompanied by an invoice.

IFPA also maintains a **mailing list** of individuals and institutions who are notified periodically of new Institute publications. Those desiring to be placed on this list should write to the Circulation Manager, Foreign Policy Reports, at the above address.

The Institute for Foreign Policy Analysis, Inc., incorporated in the Commonwealth of Massachusetts, is a tax-exempt organization under Section 501(c)(3) of the U.S. Internal Revenue Code, and has been granted status as a publicly-supported, nonprivate organization under Section 509(a)(1). Contributions to the Institute are tax-deductible.

Library of Congress Cataloging in Publication Data

Roche, John Pearson, 1923-
    The history and impact of Marxist-Leninist organizational theory.

    (Foreign policy report)
    "April 1984"—Verso t.p.
    Includes bibliographical references.
    1. Communist parties—History. 2. Communism—History. 3. Marx, Karl, 1818-1883. 4. Lenin, Vladimir Il'ich, 1870-1924. I. Title. II. Series.
HX36.R595 1984 324.1 84-4582

ISBN 0-89549-059-5

Price: $7.50

Copyright © 1984 by the
Institute for Foreign Policy Analysis, Inc.

Library of Congress Catalog Card Number: 84-4582
First Edition

First Printing
Printed by Corporate Press, Inc., Washington, D.C.

Contents

Preface

This study may be distinctive for one thing alone: it has been in gestation for almost forty-five years. As will be noted, it draws extensively on my personal experience since 1938, when, at age fifteen, I abandoned my father's Coughlinite politics and became a Norman Thomas Socialist, a member of the Young People's Socialist League. Endowed, through no efforts of my own, with a photographic memory and infinite curiosity, I was always both an activist and a clinical observer of activism. Coming from a political tradition which emphasized decisions far more than conclusions, I was perpetually bemused by the elaborate process of ratiocination most Socialists employed to justify what often to me appeared obvious.

Sometime in 1939 I observed, for example, that the Trotskyists were "agents of a non-existent foreign power." My Trotskyist contemporaries took fierce umbrage at what they considered a capitalist calumny, but in fact the Statutes of Trotsky's Fourth International, adopted in September 1938, were a mirror image of those of the Comintern, Stalin's Third International. The distinction was, as theologians say, ecclesialogical, not theological: Trotsky set himself up in business as an anti-pope.

Similarly, while I thought Karl Marx was a brilliant political journalist— his commentaries on French politics, British rule in India, and the American Civil War are *tours de force*—I never took him seriously as a prophet. All my life I have argued that one has to earn the right to hold an opinion, so I plunged into *Capital*, not just volume one which Marx wrote, but two, pieced together by Engels, and three, mainly the synoptic work of Karl Kautsky. I reached the conclusion that Marx had been left behind like a whale on a sandbar by the development of industrial capitalism, and developed a life-long admiration for "Edi" Bernstein, the German Social Democrat, who had the courage in his 1899 work *Evolutionary Socialism* to say so.

Marx, it seemed to me, had wholly missed the impact of the rise of the modern corporation on the nature of "property," largely because he never seriously analyzed developments in British industrial organization that followed the changes in the Companies Act passed by Parliament in the 1850s. (In the second volume of *Capital*, Engels unearthed evidence that Marx was vaguely aware of the thrust of limited liability expansion, but he never focused upon it.) In other words, I considered the diagnosis made by A. A. Berle and Gardner Means in *The Modern Corporation and Private Property* accurate and therefore risked excommunication from the Young People's Socialist League for opposing "nationalization of the commanding heights of industry" as the nostrum for capitalist inequities.

If you begin with the thesis that ownership equals control, nationalizing, say, the railroads would, as in Marx's perspective, eliminate the power of the "robber barons." But when you look at the reality, the stockholders do not control the corporations; the managers do. To make a long story short, I wound up arguing that to define socialism as public ownership of the means of production and distribution would simply replace a private bureaucracy with a probably more irresponsible public one.

In this intellectual journey I was immensely influenced by a strange polymath, Max Nomad, whose 1932 work, *Rebels and Renegades*, called my attention to the writings of an obscure Russian-Polish Socialist, Waclaw Machajski, who is his 1898 essay, *The Evolution of Social Democracy*, anticipated the concept of Marxism producing a "new class." Nomad's book also introduced me to the German, Robert Michels, who in 1911 published his analysis, translated as *Political Parties*, which argued for the "iron law of oligarchy"—that, in the Socialist context, the proletariat's function was not to rule, but to provide a basis of legitimation for an intellectual elite.

Later, while in graduate school at Cornell, I had the demanding pleasure of working with Michels' son-in-law, Professor Mario Einaudi, another polymath. I was plunged into the depths of elite theory and became a devotee of that elemental Sicilian Gaetano Mosca whose *Ruling Class* (a terrible translation of *classa politica*) has profoundly influenced my teaching and research in political theory and comparative politics over the past thirty-five years.

This set of convictions made me highly suspect as an orthodox Socialist, but it did open my eyes to the morphology of organizations. I was particularly impressed by the way the Stalinists, in the wake of the Stalin-Hitler Pact, managed to execute a disciplined "To the rear, march!" in such organizations as the American Student Union, the American League for Peace and Democracy, and the National Negro Congress. Through the end of August 1939, these Communist party (CP) fronts had led the demands for American involvement in the struggle against Nazism; suddenly, in the words of a parody (included on the record "Ballads for Sectarians"), "Volga boatmen sailed the Rhine."

Upon my return from military service I went to Cornell for my doctorate and immediately became involved in campus politics. It sometimes seemed in the period 1946-49 that I was out five nights a week fighting off Stalinist attempts (the old CP front, the American Student Union, was born again as American Youth for Democracy) to pass resolutions in various organizations condemning the Truman Doctrine, the Marshall

Plan, the firing of Henry Wallace, and the repressive nature of American society.

Those were frantic times: we were successfully defeating a Stalinist effort to control the American Veterans' Committee; forming Americans for Democratic Action; calling for the CIO to split from the Stalinist labor front, the World Federation of Trade Unions; doing a number on the Progressive Party and that paradigm of "useful idiots," Henry A. Wallace; and, last but not least, earning degrees and getting married.

I have discussed this era briefly in my reminiscence, "The Way Some of Us Were: Cornell, 1946-49" (*National Review*, February 5, 1982), and will only add that the commitment to anti-totalitarian activism that began in 1938, and was honed in the immediate postwar period, became a lifetime commitment, symbolized by my election as National Chairman of Americans for Democratic Action (ADA) for an unprecedented three terms (1962-65). Of course, I was also a university teacher and administrator throughout this period, first at Haverford College and then at Brandeis University.

In 1966, President Lyndon Johnson asked me to join his top White House staff as Special Consultant to the President. I accepted, and apparently, in light of its later bizarre behavior, took ADA's traditional principles with me.

In 1973, I moved from Brandeis University to The Fletcher School of Law and Diplomacy at Tufts University. I have found the academic environment here, where size makes true collegiality with both faculty colleagues and a crew of remarkable students possible, delightful, and intellectually rewarding.

In this context, I want to thank my research assistants, Sheila Peters and Richard Callow, for their assistance especially in tracking down such items as "a book by Adolph Sturmthal on Marxism in the European labor movement that I *think* was translated from German in the late 1940s."

Also I want to convey my deep appreciation to my staff assistant, Jean Callahan, who patiently responded to my obscure existential requests: "Jean, I want to add Hans Gerth's book on The Hague Conference of 1872 to footnote 27; Richard can get the exact citation. Oh, and there's a circumflex missing over the "o" in *Drole* in the citation, somewhere, of Rossi's book on the French Communist party during the *Drôle de Guerre*."

To my wife, Connie, who shared this trip since we met at a meeting of the Cornell Chapter of the Student League for Industrial Democracy in 1946, there is little I can say: our shared universe of values and affection makes words superfluous.

John P. Roche
March 1984

Summary Overview

Most analyses of Marxism-Leninism are philosophical exercises conducted in the intellectual stratosphere. This approach has a limited utility, but is based on a deeply flawed premise: that Marxism-Leninism is a form of high theory, rather than an operational code for a new-style Mafia, far more interested in finding a rationale for seizing or wielding power than in liberating "prisoners of starvation" or the "wretched of the earth."

While conservative and liberal oracles often agree that we are engaged in "a war of ideas" with the Marxist-Leninists, the hard reality is that we confront a Moscow-supported *apparat* which utilizes AK-47s, T-72 tanks, and assorted ordnance, not copies of *The Communist Manifesto*, or Lenin's *State and Revolution*, in its evangelical missions. No South Vietnamese, Salvadoran, Israeli, or American soldier has ever been killed by stepping on a copy of Marx's *Capital*.

It therefore is vital to explore the historical background of Marxism-Leninism at the operational, not the rhetorical, level. And such an investigation reveals a spectacular record of what Lenin proudly called "opportunism," of attacking targets of opportunity at whatever cost in ideological consistency or doctrinal purity.

This ruthlessness has often been considered Lenin's contribution, but Marx also knew when to "rise above principle," as he demonstrated by denouncing his opponent Ferdinand Lassalle as a "Jewish Nigger," and labeling the elemental anarchist Michael Bakunin a "Czarist agent" on evidence he knew to be forged. Each was an impediment to Marx's messianic pretensions; hence, they had to be destroyed by any available techniques, however odious. Lenin and Stalin were Marx's legitimate heirs.

The position of socialism in the world shifted in 1919 from the essentially moderate, democratic goals of the Second International to the revolutionary elitism of Lenin's Third International, or Comintern. The Social Democratic parties never recovered from their inability to prevent World War I, and from subsequently supporting their own national causes, and Lenin moved into the vacuum created by their collapse.

The Comintern, visualized in 1919 by its Soviet creators as the "General Staff of the World Revolution," operated across the globe until 1943, when Stalin—to impress President Roosevelt with his democratic bona fides—abolished it, eliminated "The International" as the Soviet national anthem, and put Commissars into pinstripe suits as "Ministers." From the time of Stalin's consolidation of power in 1927-1929, the Comintern's revolutionary mission was clearly subordinated to his perception of Soviet worldwide interests: it became an instrument of Soviet foreign policy.

In short, the "Cold War" did not begin when Winston Churchill in March 1946 made a speech in Fulton, Missouri, vividly describing Soviet activities in Eastern Europe. It began with the creation of the Comintern in 1919 and it has continued under the auspices of the International Department of the Soviet Central Committee.

However, the real legacy of Marxism-Leninism is not substantive; by all objective standards the Comintern was a disaster-area with no significant accomplishments on its record. By the time it was abolished, its meretricious behavior—switching from a tactical coalition with Hitler, to militant anti-Fascism and collective security, then back to a strategic coalition with Hitler in the space of six years—brought only contempt from authentic radicals.

Rather, what the Leninist tradition provided was an organizational model, based on the dictatorship of an enlightened "vanguard," which was adopted both by noncommunist political movements (the KMT in China, the APRA in Peru, the VNQDD in Vietnam, and various authoritarian groups in the Third World) and by "new class" cliques within the Western democracies.

These "new class" formations lack the discipline Lenin and his acolytes felt essential; indeed, they are motivated by narcissism which has been transformed into an ideology. To have a "general headquarters" issuing orders would be a demeaning ego-blow, an affront to their existential integrity. However, their "long march through the institutions" is characterized by a Leninist talent for spotting the key slots in the societal table of organization and moving into them. In the United States we have seen this "networking" phenomenon at the staff level in Congress, the Executive, the Judiciary, and public and private bureaucracies.

It is less than a conspiracy, but more than an accident, that "new class" attitudes, notably an almost aesthetic anti-Americanism, suffuse the media elite. Lenin would be horrified by the noise and sybaritic tumult, but one can argue that he was born-again at Woodstock.

1.
Communist Operational Strategies: Marx to the Sixth Comintern Congress

I T IS HARD to pick up a paper or journal without encountering the "Marxist-Leninists" at work in some obscure corner of the earth. The Indonesians, for example, have been accused of massacring thousands of Marxist-Leninist primitive tribesmen in East Timor, Ethiopian Colonel Mengistu Haile Mariam is hailed as an ideologue of this persuasion, and one suspects that when he failed an exam on Lenin's *State and Revolution*, Somalia's President Siad Barre shifted to a pro-Western posture. From this one might deduce that in every remote village, as well as in the slums and barrios of cities, diligent activists are reading Marx's *Capital*, *The Communist Manifesto*, and *Critique of the Gotha Program*, and then moving on to Lenin's *Imperialism* and *Leftwing Communism*.

In short, as the cliché puts it, we are engaged in a war of ideas with a worldwide organization of dedicated ideologues. Nothing in fact could be further from the truth. True, there are and always have been dedicated intellectuals weaned on Marx and Lenin, but they have been notable for their "unreliability" in the eyes of the party cadres. For example, when the German Communist Party (KPD), on instructions from the Sixth Congress of the Communist International (Comintern), i.e., Stalin, announced that Social Democracy, not Nazism, was the main enemy, the intellectuals wavered.

With Hitler's goons openly attempting to destroy the fragile democratic foundations of the Weimar Republic, the sensible line of action for the KPD was to form a united front with the powerful Social Democrats (SPD) against fascism, not to chant *"durch Hitler kommen wir"*—roughly, through Hitler we will achieve power. Those advocating a united front, however, were denounced as "Trotskyites" and expelled.[1] Later, when at the Seventh Congress of the Comintern in 1935 Stalin called for a united front against Hitler, those expelled were not honored for their prescience.

Why not? Here we get to the heart of the argument: they remained "traitors" because they violated party discipline. As one of the characters in Arthur Koestler's powerful *Darkness at Noon* observed, "you cannot be

---

[1] See generally Ruth Fisher, *Stalin and German Communism* (Cambridge, Mass.: Harvard University Press, 1948). For an eye-witness account by the wife of one purged KPD leader, see Margaret Buber-Neumann, *Kriegschauplätze der Weltrevolution* (Stuttgart, 1967).

right against the party." Indeed, Trotsky may be taken as the quintessential heretic. Not that he believed in freedom of opinion: the Calvinists burned heretics with the same vigor as the Spanish Inquisition, and Trotsky was as dictatorial a disciplinarian as Stalin.

No, Trotsky's mortal sin was that he combined a rejection of party discipline with an uncanny record of predicting Stalin's disasters. A couple of instances will suffice: he opposed Stalin's China policy of amalgamating the Communists with the Nationalist Kuomintang. (A remnant of this epoch is that Chiang Kai-shek's son, now President of the Republic of China on Taiwan, was educated in Moscow and has a Russian wife.) Trotsky privately circulated a document indicating the Nationalists would suddenly butcher the Communists.[2] They did—as brilliantly chronicled by André Malraux in his novel *Man's Fate*, whose main protagonist was the late Chou En-lai, thinly disguised—and Stalin blamed Trotsky!

Berthold Brecht, in a strange work, *The Measures Taken*, has also provided a gloss of the role of discipline, with the Chinese Communist ambiance as background. It is an intriguing play because, at once, it can be hailed by the faithful as a paean to "socialist realism," while on another level it can be interpreted as a savage parody of what Lenin called "democratic centralism."

Similarly, Trotsky viewed the 1928 "turn to the left" by the Comintern Congress as egregious and dangerous folly.[3] He was not in principle opposed to shooting Social Democrats—he had done a good bit of that at Kronstadt and in suppressing the democratic Transcaucasian Republics (Georgia, Armenia, and Azerbaijan) in 1921—but there was a time and a place for everything. Hitler had to be eliminated before the Social Democrats could be disposed of, and cooperation with the SPD was essential in handling that priority item.[4] When Hitler was named Chancellor by a coalition in 1933—contrary to rumor, his party never came close to an electoral majority—Trotsky immediately blew the whistle and called on Stalin to launch a preemptive military attack on Germany.[5]

Instead of cooperating with History as the "death rattle of decadent German capitalism" and providing a trampoline for the KPD to attain power, Hitler consolidated his hold on the nation with sanguinary effi-

---

[2]See Isaac Deutscher, *The Prophet Unarmed: Trotsky, 1921-1929* (London: Oxford University Press, 1959), pp. 327 ff.

[3]See *ibid.*, p. 425, discussing Trotsky's critique. It should be noted that Trotsky's initial reaction to the Sixth Congress of the Comintern was to assume that Bukharin and the right-wingers, so-called, had taken over. Subsequently, he broadened his criticism.

[4]See Isaac Deutscher, *The Prophet Outcast: Trotsky, 1929-1940* (London: Oxford University Press, 1963), p. 131.

[5]*Ibid.*, p. 214.

ciency. The vaunted power of the KPD collapsed almost overnight and the party's leaders were murdered, imprisoned, or fled to Paris and Moscow (where, ironically, most of them were later shot by Stalin). Their crime? They had obeyed his orders and since he was infallible in his analyses of the "correlation of forces," they must have bungled proper implementation of the party line.

Put another way, they were witnesses to his stupidity and the penalty for that was a bullet in the back of the neck. Or, in Trotsky's case, sending Ramon Mercader all the way to Mexico to drive an ice ax into the arch-witness's skull. But it should be emphasized again that while Trotsky was as good a Leninist as Stalin in demanding *partinost*—enforced unity—he was simply inferior to Stalin as an analyst of the "correlation of forces." When a group of American Trotskyists objected in 1940 to Trotsky's support for Stalin's invasion of Finland, they were summarily excommunicated.[6]

As we shall discuss at some length, Stalin was a worthy successor to Lenin. He was not an aberration as suggested by a number of scholars, notably Roy A. Medvedev in *Let History Judge*. Certainly, Stalin's style was antithetical to Lenin's: Lenin was an ascetic, tightly controlled personality; Stalin was a crude, jolly butcher who enjoyed a sybaritic environment.

Perhaps it gives us an interesting insight into Trotsky's failure to match Stalin at dirty infighting to note Trotsky's contempt for the man *qua* man. Stalin's filthy jokes nauseated Trotsky. The blatant anti-intellectualism—not too thinly veiled anti-Semitism—led Trotsky to underestimate the Georgian's extraordinary organizational talent and total ruthlessness. No mean egoist, Trotsky could not conceive that this clod, thrown onto the stage of history by the force of events in Petrograd at the time of the democratic revolution in February 1917 (March in the Gregorian calendar), was a threat to himself or to the old Bolshevik cadres.

Marxism-Leninism as it developed under Lenin, Stalin, Khrushchev, and Brezhnev was not a corpus of ideas. It was an organizational theory, which the Mafia must envy, devised to enhance the power of an elite working in the historical framework of Russian self-interest. When President Eisenhower's Secretary of Defense, Charles Wilson (formerly President of General Motors), observed "what was good for General Motors was good for the U.S., and vice versa," he was ridiculed. However, the

---

[6]Trotsky supported the Stalin-Hitler Pact and the Soviet invasion of Finland on essentially strategic grounds. This led to a division within the American Trotskyist movement with the leader of the Socialist Worker's Party, James Cannon, supporting Trotsky, and a minority, led by Max Shachtman, leaving the party and establishing the Workers' Party. "Cannonites" followed Trotsky in believing that the Soviet Union was a degenerate workers' state; Shachtman argued that it was a bureaucratic collectivist society with no traces of socialist theory. See Shachtman's *The Bureaucratic Revolution: The Rise of the Stalinist State* (New York: Donald Press, 1962).

proposition that what was good for Stalin, Khrushchev, Brezhnev, or Andropov was good for the Soviet Union was simply taken for granted by the Soviet elite.

To put it starkly, Marxism-Leninism is not a body of ideas designed to save the "wretched of the earth" from poverty, oppression and imperialism. It is a cynical rationale for gangsterism. Two anecdotes from the Soviet Union make the point graphically: ideals are worthless. The first, which dates back to Stalin's great purges of the 1930s, has three men meeting in a camp, a high-level "isolator." One asks the others, "Why are you here?" The first replies, "I was sentenced for conspiring against Nikolai Bukharin, head of the Comintern." The second: "I was sentenced for conspiring with Bukharin against Stalin and Comintern cadres." The questioner wryly observes, "I am Bukharin." Before one weeps for Bukharin, who has been portrayed as something of a Franciscan in recent years, it should be recalled he once observed that the Soviets believed in a two-party system: one in office, the other in jail.[7]

The second, drawn from Aleksandr Solzhenitsyn's *Gulag Archipelago*, tells of a cattle car en route to Gulag in 1945 full of convicted "enemies of the state." A guard asks one of the "zeks" how many years he got. The sentenced man says, "Twenty-five." "For what?," inquires the guard. "For nothing," says the bitter, doomed man. "Come on," says the guard, "for nothing you get only ten years."

The same bland cynicism dominated Soviet foreign policy. In 1935, French Foreign Minister Pierre Laval, later an eminent collaborator with the Nazis during the World War II Pétain regime, went to Moscow to sign a French-Soviet friendship treaty. Up to that time, the French Communist (PCF) Senators and Deputies in Parliament had ferociously opposed all defense appropriations, and Laval asked Stalin what should be done if they continued their opposition. Stalin simply ran his finger across his throat, although he privately knew that PCF leaders Maurice Thorez and Jacques Duclos would take the hint.[8] By the next defense appropriations debate in the Chamber of Deputies, the Communists were transmogrified into super-patriots.[9]

Similarly, in the years 1945-48, when the Yugoslav Communists were more Stalinist than Stalin, Milovan Djilas, then Tito's top aide who has

---

[7]See the recent attempt at rehabilitation of Bukharin by Stephen Cohen in his biography, *Bukharin and the Bolshevik Revolution: A Political Biography, 1888-1938* (New York: A.A. Knopf, 1973).

[8]Arthur Koestler reports this in his *The Invisible Writing* (Boston: Beacon Press, 1954; paperback edition), p. 325.

[9]For a remarkable exploration of the degree to which Maurice Thorez and the other communist leaders became super-patriots, see chapters 18 and 19 in Gérard Walter, *Histoire du Parti Communiste Français* (Paris: Aimery Somogy, 1948).

since become a dissident, inquired in Moscow what Belgrade should do about the bizarre Albanian Communists. Stalin, with a vivid gesture, said, "Gobble them up." Djilas was a bit startled, but Molotov reiterated, "Gobble them up."[10] Without going into detail, it is clear that Moscow later supported French President Charles De Gaulle's policy of independence from the United States and sandbagged Socialist candidate François Mitterrand in the Presidential election of 1965. One can be sure the vulpine Mitterrand (known as "the Florentine") has not forgotten, despite his cooperation with the PCF.

The classic act of cynical expedience was, of course, the Nazi-Soviet Pact of August 1939. There was a Kafkaesque quality about the whole scenario: a Nazi military band greeting Molotov in Berlin with the "International," and Soviet musical reciprocity when Ribbentrop, Hitler's Foreign Minister, arrived in Moscow to the strains of "Deutschland Über Alles" and the "Horst Wessel Song." Various pundits have tried to justify Stalin's action as defensive, but that does not hold up under close scrutiny: the time he allegedly "bought" was wholly wasted. Indeed, instead of strengthening their defenses, the Soviets lowered their guard.

The British and French had been seeking a Soviet alliance for roughly a year. It is fair to say that the idea was not cherished by the Chamberlain Government or the traditional elite, but even if the British delegation to Moscow had been led by, say, Harry Pollit—head of the British Communist Party—he would have thought the Soviet conditions impossible.

In essence, Moscow demanded hegemony over Estonia, Latvia, Lithuania, Bessarabia, Finland, and much of Poland. Hitler and Ribbentrop had no problems with this; no parliamentary opposition would scream its head off about national honor, betrayal of small nations, and related moral questions. But for the British and French such a deal would have been suicidal to their democratic systems. Oddly enough, Hitler seems to have been the only person Stalin trusted: the Soviet dictator was delighted with a treaty which, he thought, would send the *Wehrmacht* west.

It has been argued that Stalin, with Machiavellian calibration, made the deal to buy time for Soviet preparations against an eventual Nazi assault. There are two problems with this explanation: First, there is no hard evidence the Soviets did utilize the time to reinforce their defenses. Second, despite British and American warnings of impending attack, derived from the "Ultra" cracking of Nazi codes in which Berlin informed Tokyo of its plans (which had been confirmed by the Kremlin's crack Tokyo agent, Richard Sorge), Stalin's reaction to the massive attack was,

---

[10]Milovan Djilas, *Conversations with Stalin* (New York: Harcourt, Brace & World, 1962), p. 143.

according to Khrushchev and Solzhenitsyn, one of betrayed disbelief.[11] The huge *Wehrmacht* buildup on the Russian front had been impossible to hide, but the Nazis—much to their amazement—achieved tactical surprise on every front.[12] Stalin had even refused to "provoke" Hitler by flying aerial reconnaissance missions over the German lines!

Let us now turn to the historical background of the Marxist-Leninist "solar system." From the day the Bolsheviks overthrew the first democratic government in Russian history, efforts were made to create an international network of satellite parties. This was formalized by the creation of the Communist or Third International—the Comintern—in 1919. In its early years, the Comintern attracted a remarkable collection of left-wing idealists to its ranks: the names of Ignazio Silone and Angelica Balabanoff, Victor Serge, and Boris Souvarine come to mind.

The Comintern's first goal was to eliminate the Second or Socialist International, founded in 1889, by capturing its component parties. We shall explore the key organizational techniques—infiltration and colonization—below. Here it is important to contrast the covert and the advertised objectives of creating the Comintern. The secret agenda was the defense of the Soviet Union. The foreign parties and their fellow travelers, whom Lenin with his characteristic bluntness called "useful idiots," were to be instruments of Soviet state policy. The left-wingers in various Socialist parties who rushed to form Communist parties may have thought their mission was to forward the proletarian world revolution. The *apparatchiks*, shorthand for Soviet party bureaucrats, looked on them as expendable cannon fodder in the cause of Soviet imperialism.

Indeed, the designation "International" was itself deceptive. The Socialist International was in fact precisely that: a body including various Socialist parties which sent delegates to conferences and engaged in free and often ferocious debate. The German SPD had a preeminent status based on its ancestors, Marx and Engels, and its enormous success in mobilizing the German workingclass behind its banner, but it could never dictate policy to the American, Italian, or any other member party.[13]

---

[11]Stalin's behavior throughout this whole period was virtually psychotic: in January 1941, for example, a copy of the actual directive for operation "Barbarossa," the invasion of the Soviet Union, prepared on December 18, 1940, was turned over to an American in Berlin by an anti-Nazi German official. It was checked out in Washington and then sent on to the Kremlin, but Stalin simply ignored it. Later, on the basis of the "Ultra" messages, that is, the breaking of the top-secret Nazi code, Winston Churchill told his ambassador in Moscow, Sir Stafford Cripps, to warn Stalin; again, this was ignored, and Cripps was publicly denounced as a provocateur.

[12]One of the most telling attacks on Stalin by Khrushchev in his "Secret Speech" of 1956 was that Stalin had literally gone into a catatonic seizure on hearing the news of the *Wehrmacht's* assault.

[13]See James Joll, *The Second International 1889-1914* (London: Weidenfeld and Nicolson, 1955), and the classic, if interminable, study, Julius Braunthal, *History of the International* (London: Gollancz, 1967, and revisions to 1980; two volumes).

In contrast, the Comintern was a wholly-owned subsidiary of the Communist Party of the Soviet Union (CPSU), whose delegates dominated every aspect of its operations, screened the staff, and made no secret of it. Foreign Communists used to scream "Foul!" when accused of being agents of the Soviet Union, but the statutes of the Comintern gave the "Center"—the Executive Committee Communist International (ECCI), always Soviet dominated—the power to overrule the decisions of any member party.[14] For example, in 1929 it expelled the majority of the American Communist Party, the "Lovestoneites," for "right-deviationism."[15] The old American axiom about politicians, "Don't listen to what he says: watch his hands," could be applied in spades to Marxist-Leninists. The organizational emphasis developed, in part, from the tradition of underground activity in Russia against the Czars; partly, it emerged from Lenin's passion for the Prussian military theorist Karl von Clausewitz; but, as we shall now see, it was also an inheritance from Karl Marx himself.

The Marxist Legacy

Karl Marx wrote surprisingly little on the subject of organization, and what little there is is largely polemical. He was, for example, convinced that the leaders of the SPD connived with the Prussian police to see that he was not permitted to return from exile. Given Marx's authoritarian temperament and total inability to accept the ground rules of any organization unless he wrote and enforced them himself, one could sympathize with the leaders of the SPD had they wished him permanently exiled. However, August Bebel, Karl Kautsky, Wilhelm Liebknecht, and Eduard Bernstein, the SPD quadrumvirate, were innocent of the charge.

In 1875, when the two existing German socialist groups—Marxists and Lassallians—met at Gotha to form a unified party, they agreed on a Program. When Marx, whom nobody consulted in his London exile,

---

[14]See *Statutes of the Communist International*, adopted at the Second Comintern Congress, August 4, 1920, item 9: "The Executive Committee conducts the entire work of the Communist International from one Congress to the next, publishes, in at least four languages, the central organ of the Communist International . . . and issues instructions which are binding on all parties and organizations belonging to the International: it shall expel groups or persons who offend against international discipline, and it also has the right to expel from the Communist International those parties which violate decisions of the world congress." Quoted in Jane Degras, *The Communist International 1919-1943: Documents* (London: Oxford University Press, for the Royal Institute of International Affairs, 1956; three volumes), Vol. 1, p. 165.

[15]The Lovestoneites were condemned after the Sixth Congress of the Comintern in 1928 as suspected Bukharinites. It was most amusing because Jay Lovestone, the leader of the American Communist Party, had just been re-elected by roughly 80 percent of the annual convention when he was suddenly expelled. This led to the joke: "Question: 'Why is the American Communist Party like the Brooklyn Bridge?' Answer: 'They both depend upon cables.'"—a reference to the message from Moscow which had disposed of Lovestone.

received an advance copy he blew up like a volcano. Without exploring the intricacies of the argument between Marx and the eccentric Ferdinand Lassalle, who had built a formidable socialist movement, the "Association of German Workers," in Prussia before he was killed in an 1864 duel, it is sufficient to note that their central conflict was over the role of the state.

Lassalle—that "Jewish nigger," in Marx's kindly phrase—had worked in covert alliance with Bismarck probably because the Prussian Prince wanted to build up the power of the industrial sector against the "Junkers," the agrarian nobility. When the Lassallians and the Marxists combined to form the SPD at Gotha there was, in fact, little friction and the Program passed almost perfunctorily.

One reason for this unity was that Marx's savage critique had been suppressed by the "Marxist" leadership at the Conference! Indeed, it was kept under wraps until 1891—eight years after Marx's death—when Engels finally published it.[16] To Marx, the Program was a sell-out; the Marxists had traded their heritage for a mess of Lassallian pottage. The "Royal Prussian Socialists" (as he once dubbed the followers of Lassalle) had captured the theoretical high ground. The gist of Marx's complaint was that "the whole program, for all its democratic clang, is tainted through and through by the servile belief in the state, or, what is no better, by democratic miracle-faith, . . . both equally remote from socialism."[17]

This strikes to the central antinomy of Marxist political theory: Were the believers in dialectical materialism to be the heirs or the assassins of capitalism?[18] In Marx's five-stage eschatology, inexorable historical forces transform the human condition. No one, not even the President of the United States Chamber of Commerce, has ever hailed capitalism with the gusto of Marx and Engels in the *Communist Manifesto*. The role of the bourgeoisie, they asserted, was to eliminate feudal obscurantism, achieve massive capital development, Westernize the benighted natives of today's

---

[16]Marx's critique of the Gotha Program, some extended correspondence between Marx and Engels on one hand and Wilhelm Bracke in Germany, Engels' introduction to the critique of the Gotha Program which finally appeared in 1891, and Lenin's extensive critique of the critique of the Gotha Program can be found in Karl Marx, *The Critique of the Gotha Programme* (New York: International Publishers, Marxist Library, 1938), Vol. II.

[17]*Ibid.*, p. 32. Marx's racial slurs were standard fare in his correspondence. The reference to Lassalle's ancestry (based partly on his swarthy appearance) is from letters to Wilhelm Liebknecht cited in Daniel Bell's classic, "Marxian Socialism in the United States," in Donald D. Egbert and Stowe Persons, editors, *Socialism and American Life* (Princeton, N.J.: Princeton University Press, 1952; two volumes), Vol. 1, p. 233.

[18]This formulation is borrowed from Adolf Sturmthal, *The Tragedy of European Labor* (New York: Columbia, 1943). It was employed by SPD leader F. Tarnow at the party's 1931 Leipzig Congress in a slightly different form.

"Third World," and put out the red carpet for the next stage of the historical drama: socialism.

Thus, recent efforts to turn Marx into a sociological critic of alienation—an exercise based on his Hegelian, Baudelaire phase in Paris—are fundamentally nonsense. The mature Marx was not a social worker: the man who could assert in *Capital* that "individuals are dealt with only insofar as they are personifications of economic categories, embodiments of particular class relations and class interests" was hardly a caring person. Marx viewed alienation, that is, the resentment felt by an oppressed class, say, the proletariat under capitalism, as a necessary concomitant of progress. A happy proletarian was, for the post-Hegelian Marx, suffering from an acute case of "false consciousness"; alienation became the badge of true class consciousness and rising revolutionary fervor, not a cause for tears and lamentations.

But what is this alienated proletarian to do to alter his tragic condition? The simple-minded realists of the SPD said, "Join a Socialist party and capture the apparatus of the capitalist state." Yet, by definition, the state for Marx was a superstructure erected on the substructure of capitalism, that is, in Marx's vivid phrase, "the executive committee of the bourgeoisie." By definition, the formation of a Marxist political party was a capitulation to the capitalist *zeitgeist*, an acceptance of the notion that politics, rather than being merely a cosmetic charade, might advance the interest of the workingclass.

The Gotha Program put forward a series of immediate demands behind which was the implicit assumption that the SPD would, as a political player, attempt to get elected to the *Reichstag* and by law implement these proposals—free universal education, child labor laws, and the like.[19] Obviously this required, at least *sub silentio*, an acceptance of the legitimacy of the capitalist state as an instrument of progressive social change. To Marx this reeked of Lassalle's state socialism, but what did he offer in its place? If the proletariat could not capture the state by political means, how could socialists get to socialism?

His response created more questions than answers. "What transformation will the state undergo in a communist society?," he asked himself, and went on: "In other words, what social functions will remain in existence there that are analogous to the present functions of the state? This question can only be answered scientifically and one does not get a flea-hop nearer to the problem by a thousand-fold combination of the word 'people' with the word 'state.'"[20]

---

[19]See the project as it is laid out for purposes of criticism of Marx, in Marx, *op. cit.*

[20]*Ibid.*, p. 18.

9

Then the scientist, whom Engels in his graveside eulogy compared to Darwin, pins the specimen and precisely defines its morphology: "Between capitalist and communist society lies the period of the revolutionary transformation of the one into the other. There corresponds to this also a political transition period in which the state can be nothing but the revolutionary dictatorship of the proletariat."[21] Well, that solves that—except for one problem: What are the instruments of the revolutionary dictatorship of the proletariat? Socialist parties? Anarchist-style general strikes? Or, in Lenin's version, a "vanguard" party literally patterned on a military commando brigade?

This ethereal definition of the revolutionary process set off a struggle among Marxists which continues in arcane fashion to this day. In general, the Socialists—led by the SPD, tacitly supported by Engels after Marx's death—defined the "revolutionary dictatorship of the proletariat" as an electoral victory by the Socialist parties. There were elaborate Talmudic disputes, mainly in France, over the degree to which the French party (SFIO) should cooperate with other progressive political groups. When the Dreyfus Case, the trial of a Jewish French Army captain for espionage, tore France apart in the 1890s, the Socialist leadership initially assumed a neutral posture: it was a private fight among the *bourgeoisie*.[22]

However, as national frenzy, triggered by Emile Zola's *J'Accuse!*, a fierce assertion that Dreyfus had been framed, polarized the country and rumors of a military coup fluttered through the bistros, the Socialists had to come to terms with reality. The great Socialist tribune Jean Jaurès broke the ice in January 1898, with a jeremiad in the Chamber of Deputies in which he savaged the Army, the Catholic Church, and the anti-Semitic Royalist Leagues. It cost him his seat in the May 1898 election, but the die was cast: the Socialists would participate in the defense of the bourgeois Republic against its reactionary elements.

As the evidence accumulated that Dreyfus had indeed been framed, the militant and powerful reactionaries, mostly royalists who never accepted the legitimacy of the Republic, brought France close to civil war. The Republicans responded by forming a broad coalition for the "Defense of the Republic," including both Socialist leader Alexandre Millerand and General Gaston de Gallifet, a Marquis, but a devoted Republican who had most recently demonstrated his military talents by brutally suppressing the Paris Commune in 1871. The Commune was sacred to the Social-

---

[21]*Ibid.*

[22]Generally see Harvey Goldberg, *The Life of Jean Jaurès* (Madison, Wisc.: University of Wisconsin Press, 1962), Part III: "Years of Anguish, 1898-1906." Also interesting is Nicholas Halasz, *Captain Dreyfus* (New York: Grove Press, 1957).

ists and the thought of Millerand working in tandem with the butcher of the Communards turned the SFIO inside out.[23]

Enough of the details. Suffice it to say this launched the great dispute over "Ministerialism" in particular, and the limits of Socialist collaboration with bourgeois political groups in general. The problem intensified with the outbreak of World War I, the inclusion of Socialists in the British and French governments, and the support for war appropriations by the SPD members of the *Reichstag*. Unfortunately, Marx left no political testament on how Marxists were to behave in their quest for the "revolutionary dictatorship of the proletariat."

If we turn to Friedrich Engels, specifically to the excerpts from his *Anti-Dühring*, published separately in 1882 as *Socialism: Utopian and Scientific*, we find a somewhat more elaborate roadmap which, oddly enough, features the state. "By more and more driving towards the conversion of the vast socialized means of production," he wrote,

into state property [the proletariat] points the way for the carrying through of the revolution. *The proletariat seizes the state power and transforms the means of production in the first instance into state property.* But in doing this, it puts an end to itself as the proletariat, it puts an end to all class differences and class antagonisms: it puts an end also to the state as the state. . . ."[24]

When ultimately it becomes representative of society as a whole, [the state] makes itself superfluous. . . . The first act in which the state really comes forward as the representative of society as a whole—the taking possession of the means of production in the name of society—is at the same time its last independent act as a state. The interference of the state power in social relations becomes superfluous in one sphere after another, and then ceases of itself.[25]

Then we reach Engels' widely quoted summary (actually borrowed from the "utopian socialist" Saint-Simon): "The government of persons is replaced by the administration of things and the direction of the processes of production. The state is not 'abolished,' *it withers away*."[26] The concept of the "withering away of the state" thus entered the Marxist lexicon, but offered little assistance to those concerned about the subjective role of Marxist political movements. Perhaps all that was required was to ride the "locomotive of history" to its last stop?

If we turn to Karl Marx's activities as a political activist, we get some clue as to his personal approach to organizational behavior. In 1864,

---

[23]See Goldberg, *op. cit.*, pp. 271 ff.

[24]Friedrich Engels, "Socialism: Utopian and Scientific," in Karl Marx, *Selected Works* (Moscow: Foreign Languages Publishing House, 1951), Vol. II, p. 138. (Italics in original.)

[25]*Ibid.*, pp. 181-182.

[26]*Ibid.* (Italics in original.)

Marx and a congeries of British and foreign radicals formed the International Working Men's Association (IWA), often styled the "First International." It was a ragtag and bobtail outfit, but attracted Michael Bakunin's anarchists like a magnetic field. These frenetic extremists formed branches in Spain, the Jura, and elsewhere, and by 1872 at the Hague Congress were on the threshold of gaining control of the IWA from the Marxists. This, of course, was intolerable to Marx, who looked on anarchism as romantic, individualistic tripe, and on Bakunin as an arrogant cretin.[27]

His solution was to move the headquarters away from London and into the care of his devoted follower, Friedrich A. Sorge in Hoboken, New Jersey. Sorge, a carpenter, prepared its coffin and a quiet burial took place in 1876. All, of course, by Marx's fiat.[28] Perhaps he and Lenin might have understood each other better than some Marxists are willing to believe. (The anarchists, correctly claiming that they had been swindled, kept up the IWA as a kind of ghost-with-letterhead. As late as the Spanish Civil War, the "Black International" was issuing ukases—though I have yet to meet anyone, except Burnett Bolloten, who ever read one.[29])

To conclude, Marx provided little insight into organizational theory. The other leading Marxists followed closely the tactics of the SPD "bonzen," party bosses like Ignaz Auer, August Bebel, and Wilhelm Liebknecht, who turned the SPD into a para-polity. Babies were brought into the world by Socialist midwives; they went to Socialist kindergartens and then to special ideological classes; they joined the Socialist Union (DAGB), belonged to Socialist stamp clubs, sports clubs, and insurance collectives; they married Party comrades, voted for Socialist *Reichstag* candidates, took their ailments to Socialist clinics, and on departure from this vale of exploitation were seen off by Socialist funerals. The SPD, in short, was a closed system, a state within a state.

The new society, to employ Marx's metaphor, was developing in the womb of the old. Although there was much revolutionary rhetoric on Holy Days of Obligation such as May Day—and Eduard Bernstein was almost excommunicated for urging the elimination of these fiery clichés—the unarticulated assumption of the SPD was that the transformation

---

[27]For a vivid description of Marx's tumultuous relationship with the leading anarchist Michael Bakunin, see E. H. Carr, *Michael Bakunin* (New York: Vintage Books, 1961; reprint of 1937 edition), Book V: "Bakunin and Marx." For a blow-by-blow examination of the 1872 Congress of the IWA, see Hans Gerth, *The First International: Minutes of the Hague Congress* (Madison, Wisc.: University of Wisconsin Press, 1958).

[28]Carr, *op. cit.*, pp. 424 ff.

[29]See Burnett Bolloten, *The Spanish Revolution* (Chapel Hill, North Carolina: University of North Carolina Press, 1979), pp. 182-198, especially p. 183, n. 2.

from capitalism to socialism would be peaceful.[30] One day the historical forces that filled God's role in Marx's worldview would give the proletariat an electoral majority, and a new epoch would dawn.

This complacent approach to the "revolutionary dictatorship of the proletariat" was challenged at various conferences of the Socialist International. Invariably, Rosa Luxemburg, who belonged both to the SPD and to the Socialist Party of the Kingdom of Poland and Lithuania (a bizarre outfit if ever there was one) would call for militance, particularly against the threat of war.[31]

Off in a corner was a group of Russians who seemed to specialize in cutting each other up and were considered a public nuisance by the Socialist magnates. Among them was a short, intense man with a distinctly central Asian cast to his aquiline features, Vladimir Ilyich Ulyanov, who took the party name of V. I. Lenin. Organization, not high theory, was his forte—and the techniques of infiltration he devised provide the central themes of this study.

Lenin's Organizational Thrust

This is not the place for an extensive biography of Lenin: readers are referred to the works of David Shub, Bertram Wolfe, and Adam Ulam.[32] However, anyone wanting to get a sense of this ruthless genius should read Aleksandr Solzhenitsyn's *Lenin in Zurich.*[33] Perhaps because Solzhenitsyn is as volcanic, single-tracked, and demonic a hater as Lenin, he has encapsulated the essence of the man in this brief, semi-fictitious volume. When Lenin entered the circle of Russian Social Democrats (RSDAP) in the early 1890s, the reigning magnates were George Plekhanov, Peter Struve, and Julius Martov. They were Marxist theoreticians with, as later events would demonstrate, little organizational talent. To them, reactionary, agrarian, Czarist Russia, then in the first stages of industrialization, was still in Marx's feudal epoch; it had yet to achieve its bourgeois revolution, for which the French Revolution of 1789 was a paradigm. Essentially, the RSDAP envisaged the role of Russian Marxists as cooperating

[30]For a brilliant study of Eduard Bernstein's fundamental critique of Marx, see Peter Gay, *The Dilemma of Democratic Socialism* (New York: Collier Books, 1962).

[31]See J. P. Nettl, *Rosa Luxemburg* (London: Oxford University Press, 1966; two volumes), Vol. II, pp. 780-781.

[32]David Shub, *Lenin* (Garden City, N.Y.: The Country Life Press, 1948); Bertram Wolfe, *Three Who Made a Revolution* (New York: Dial Press, 1948); Adam Ulam, *The Bolsheviks* (New York: Macmillan, 1965). For further detail on the internal developments within the party at a later date, Leonard Schapiro, *The Communist Party of the Soviet Union* (New York: Random House, Vintage, 1971; second edition) is invaluable.

[33](New York: Farrar, Straus and Giroux, 1976).

with progressive elements of the bourgeoisie to achieve a Russian 1789.[34]

When Lenin reached St. Petersburg in 1893, he rose rapidly in the Socialist circle. It was a personal, rather than a philosophical, emergence: throughout his life, Lenin was a savage anti-intellectual. True, he had to get his intellectual credentials as a Marxist and later did so with an impenetrable work entitled *Materialism and Empirio Criticism* (1909). What this work lacks in philosophical mass is more than compensated for by the energy with which Lenin lashed out personally against all those who, in his eyes, had deviated from Marxist truth.

To read the memoirs of his associates in that era, most of whom he subsequently consigned to the "dustbin of history," makes it clear they never knew what hit them. One can speculate that these closet philosophers of the 1890s were impressed and intimidated by the stern, brutal frankness and action-orientation of this potential land mine. To change the metaphor, he resembled a grenade with the pin pulled and no way to know how soon the blast would occur.

To compress the historical narrative, Lenin was arrested and exiled to Siberia whence he departed for Europe in 1900. Fifteen of his next seventeen years were spent in one city or another where fellow Russian exiles gathered in their favorite restaurants, drank glasses of tea, and conspired against the Czar and each other. Lenin, as purposeful as ever, had two major objectives: first, to unify the Russian Socialists under his leadership, and, second, to get a newspaper of his own, an essential component of any communications network in the era before radio and television.

Implicit in all his activities was the assumption that—despite Marx's view in his *Preface to the Critique of Political Economy* (1859) that "no social order ever perishes before all the productive forces for which there is room in it have developed; and new, higher relations of production never appear before the material conditions of their existence have matured in the womb of the old society itself"—somehow or other, feudal Russia could be transformed into a socialist state without going through the seemingly endless process of capitalist development. That is, that History could be shortcut. He took various theoretical stabs at this problem of speeding the locomotive of History—notably in *What is to be Done?* (1902) and *Two Tactics of Social Democracy in the Democratic Revolution* (1905)— but they were pretty shoddy. It remained for "Parvus" (Alexander Helphand) and his disciple Leon Trotsky to square the Marxist circle with the theory of "permanent revolution."[35]

---

[34]The best description of Lenin in this period is Wolfe, *op. cit.*

[35]See the biography of Alexander Helphand by Z.A.B. Zeman and W. B. Scharlau, *The Merchant of*

Meanwhile, Lenin went about the task of unifying and capturing the Russian social democracy. A Unity Congress was scheduled for July 1903 in Brussels, and Lenin set to work early to pack the house. "The composition of the Party Congress was settled in advance," Lenin said, "by [his] Organization Committee."[36] He was quite happy to turn the programmatic side over to George Plekhanov, and the Program was in fact adopted unanimously (with one abstention). Then the Congress got down to Lenin's hidden agenda: the Party rules. When, in mid-debate, the Belgian police began to arrest various delegates, the whole, interrupted Congress packed up and moved to London—arguing all the way.

The battle over the Party rules hinged on Lenin's concept of a "vanguard" directing the membership along military lines of command. As one opponent put it: "Is not Lenin dreaming of the administration of an entire party by a few guardians of doctrine?"[37] The answer was, "Yes." Lenin, thinking against the background of Czarist tyranny, wanted a conspiratorial, thoroughly disciplined cadre. On the other hand, Julius Martov, essentially drawing on the SPD model, considered party membership a simple matter: one joined, paid dues, elected officers, and waited for History to fulfill its mission in Russia. The brawl went on from August 11 to 23, day and night.

Lenin's manipulations finally won the day. He was helped by the idealism of some of his opponents who did not share his fondness for "opportunism" and walked out on principle. It was psychologically important because the Leninists then forever designated themselves the "Bolsheviks," or majority, while their opponents, who in fact had a far larger constituency, went into history as the "Mensheviks," or minority. In the long run, the lesson Communists learned from the "Unity Congress" was to let the ideologues play with the Platform Committee but keep an iron grip on the Credentials Committee. Although Plekhanov was shortly to break with Lenin, his Program remained the Party's official formulation until after the Bolshevik Revolution.

Thus began the era of appalling internecine warfare within the Russian Socialist movement. The various groups plagued the Second International, mostly with complaints about the Leninists. For example, there were objections that the latter condoned bank robberies to finance Party activities: Stalin got his start at this trade, and Maxim Litvinov first appeared on the stage of History when he walked into a Paris bank with a suitcase full of stolen rubles and asked to have them converted into

Revolution: The Life of Alexander Israel Helphand (Parvus) 1867-1924 (Oxford: Oxford University Press, 1965).

[36]Cited by Wolfe, *op. cit.*, p. 232.

[37]This was the veteran Social Democrat Paul Axelrod, cited in *ibid.*, p. 241.

francs. To the International this was outrageous and the practice was severely censured.[38]

There was an interesting exchange at the International Socialist Conference at Copenhagen in 1910. As usual, there was an effort to sort out the interminable fights in the Russian movement, and a member of the International Socialist Bureau asked Paul Axelrod, veteran Menshevik,

> "Do you mean to say that all these splits and quarrels and scandals are the work of one man? But how can one man be so effective and so dangerous?"

> Axelrod: "Because there is not another man who for twenty-four hours of the day is taken up with the revolution, who has no other thoughts but thoughts of revolution, and who, even in his sleep, dreams of revolution. Just try and handle such a fellow."[39]

Trotsky, who had worked with Lenin at the 1903 Congress, soon broke and denounced the "egocentralism" of the Party rules: "The organization of the Party takes the place of the Party itself; the Central Committee takes the place of the organization; and finally the dictator takes the place of the Central Committee."[40] This was an accurate definition of Lenin's "democratic centralism," and prophetic in anticipating Stalinist Russia.

Despite the deceptive designation "Mensheviks," the mainstream of Russian social democratic thought still saw Russia as, at best, on the threshold of the bourgeois revolution which would bring capitalism to power. Lenin had to find a rationale for telescoping the capitalist revolution into the socialist epoch. He also had to find a Marxist explanation for revolutionary agitation in a backward agrarian state populated by illiterate peasants, with a minuscule workingclass.

To oversimplify, the scheme he improvised was based on the English economist J. A. Hobson's *Imperialism*, Rudolph Hilferding's *Finance Capital*, some random comments by Marx and Engels on the Irish question in which they suggested a revolutionary Irish peasantry could ignite the British industrial workingclass, and the "Parvus"-Trotsky theory of permanent revolution or combined development.[41] World War I he saw as

---

[38]Lenin took the position now held by a number of assorted terrorists that to rob a bank is to strike a blow against capitalism. The Second International found that Bolshevik addiction to "expropriation" scandalous, and held various hearings on the subject at which Lenin generally downplayed his formal support. In Stockholm, in 1906, the Conference of the Second International formally forbade expropriations and ordered the dissolution of all bodies engaged in such activity and the expulsion of all "expropriators." Lenin simply backed off and refused to attend the session at which the vote was taken. See *ibid.*, pp. 371 ff.

[39]Quoted in *ibid.*, p. 249.

[40]Cited in *ibid.*, p. 253.

[41]J. A. Hobson, *Imperialism* (New York: J. Pott & Company, 1902); Ralph Fox, *Marx, Engels and Lenin on Ireland* (New York: International Publishers, 1940); see also my discussion of this in John P. Roche, *Shadow and Substance* (New York: Macmillan, 1964), "The Case of Victor Serge," pp. 280 ff.

16

the death rattle of capitalism, which had become a worldwide rather than merely a national phenomenon: the internal contradictions and struggle for markets led to a war and the task of revolutionaries was to find the "weak link" in the capitalist chain.

If this link could be broken, the revolution would be contagious and capitalism as a whole would be consigned to the historical graveyard. Now if we factor in the role of the revolutionary agrarians in triggering the proletarian uprising, we begin to see the model: a Bolshevik revolt in Russia would ignite the German workers. Enter "Parvus"-Trotsky: once the Russian and German people had overthrown their authoritarian regimes, the two would go forward arm in arm, with the Bolsheviks providing the revolutionary consciousness and the German Communists the primitive capital development and technology transfer necessary to industrialize Russia. Capitalism would be built in Russia by socialist means— there would be no capitalist class.

Thus, the whole success or failure of the Bolshevik Revolution was initially premised on a German revolution. As Lenin said to the Seventh Party Congress in 1918, "It is an absolute fact that without the German Revolution we must perish. . . . No matter what the development may be, should the German revolution fail to take place, we must perish."[42] With the failure of the abortive Spartacus revolt in Berlin in the winter of 1918-19, Lenin—like many other millenarians before him—went back to the astrologer and recalculated the time-frame. A German revolution was still essential in theory, but in practice all hands, Trotsky included, moved toward "Socialism in One Country."

Viewed objectively, the Russian Revolution had roughly as much to do with Marx's "revolutionary dictatorship of the proletariat" as did the latest coup in Bolivia or Benin. (The Italian Marxist theorist Antonio Gramsci flatly, and approvingly, stated in 1917, "the Bolsheviks reject Karl Marx."[43]) Ironically, it was the antithesis of Marx's whole conception of the supremacy of the economic over the political. Lenin and Trotsky, two organizational geniuses, extremely well-funded by the German General Staff which considered them reliable agents to destabilize Russia, seized power from an unseasoned, divided democratic regime led by Alexander Kerensky.[44] Lenin managed to infiltrate several parties in the Kerensky coalition, notably the Social Revolutionaries, exacerbating inner

---

[42]See V. I. Lenin, *Selected Works* (Moscow: Foreign Languages Publishing House, 1947), Vol. II, pp. 299-300.

[43]See "The Revolution Against Capital," *L'Avanti!* (Milan), November 24, 1917.

[44]See Michael Pearson, *The Sealed Train* (New York: Putnam, 1975).

disarray. "Power," said Lenin, "was lying in the streets and we picked it up. It was light as a feather."[45]

Once in power, Lenin lost no time in creating international organizations to agitate abroad on behalf of the Bolshevik Government. He was able to capitalize on war weariness and cynicism in the European working-class to launch takeover bids for the Social Democratic parties. Despite anti-war programs before 1914, the Socialist parties in every belligerent state except Italy and the United States supported their nations' actions. From his refuge in Zurich, Lenin had thundered at these traitors, these "social patriots," and had called for transforming the imperialist war into revolution.[46]

In the spirit of bitter disillusionment that was the hangover from the "Great War" (someone called it "the second Fall of Man"), Lenin's message had considerable appeal. The SPD had already split into pro- and anti-war factions by 1917, and the Leninists peeled off from the essentially anti-militarist USPD (Independent Social Democratic Party) to form the *Spartacusbund* in combination with Rosa Luxemburg's non-Leninist revolutionary partisans.[47] It was they who, over Luxemburg's objections, launched the *putsch* in January 1919, which was brutally suppressed by the para-military *Freikorps*.

Luxemburg was the only competition Lenin had on the international socialist Left—she was a brilliant analyst and an authentic Marxist intellectual—and there is some reason to believe Lenin had a hand in her murder by the *Freikorps*. Among other things, she was militantly opposed to German socialists getting mixed up in Lenin's planned Communist International. At any rate, Wilhelm Pieck, a young Spartacist, was captured with her and Karl Liebknecht in a supposed "safe house." Luxemburg and Liebknecht were brutally murdered, while Pieck was freed without even the ritual *Freikorps* beating. Pieck became a devoted Stalinist (with his crony Walter Ulbricht), a survivor of Stalin's purge of former KPD (German Communist Party) cadres who had taken "refuge" in the

---

[45]He developed this theme at length in his "Political Report of the Central Committee" to the Extraordinary Seventh Congress of the Russian Communist Party (Bolsheviks), March 7, 1918. It created some problems for later historians who wanted to dramatize the ferocity of the Great Soviet Revolution.

[46]See his "Opportunism and the Collapse of the Second International," "The War Program of the Proletarian Revolution," and "Imperialism" in Lenin, *op. cit.*, Vol. 1, pp. 607-734.

[47]See Nettl, *op. cit.*, Vol. II, pp. 706-736. Also interesting is the memoir of her close friend, Paul Frölich, *Rosa Luxemburg: Her Life and Work* (London: Gollancz, 1940). In prison in 1916, Rosa Luxemburg wrote a brief pamphlet entitled "The Russian Revolution," which was prophetic in its anticipation of later developments arising from Lenin's concept of the nature of the revolutionary party. She was completely opposed to Lenin's cooperation with the Kaiser's military forces in the effort to achieve power, and felt that it was unethical and that it indicated Lenin's subservience to "Parvus" or Alexander Helphand. (Nettl, *op. cit.*, Vol. II, pp. 634 ff.) Out of respect for Luxemburg's memory, the German Communist Party refused to agree to the formation of the Comintern in 1919.

USSR, and, eventually, the first President of the German Democratic Republic (East Germany). He was accused in 1929 of betraying Luxemburg and Liebknecht and brought to trial by a KPD "Court of Honor," but Stalin suppressed the whole matter.[48] Rough play in international communism began early.

The major instrument for coordinating the work of the Communist parties worldwide was the Communist International, "the General Staff of the World Revolution." Mention has already been made of the subordination of national parties to the Comintern's directives, but a further sense of the organizational emphasis can be gained from Zinoviev's famous "Twenty-One Demands."[49] Gregory Zinoviev was Lenin's man at the Comintern and at other foreign ventures such as the Baku Congress of the Toilers of the East; he did not write a sentence without clearing it with Lenin.

The background of this set of specifications for membership in the Comintern was almost total chaos in the world Socialist movement. The Second International had been disrupted and discredited by the War, and everywhere one looked Socialist parties were splitting and requesting admission to the Comintern. The American Socialist Party, for instance, gave birth to two Communist parties, each of which applied for admission, and then requested membership for itself.[50] When we get to Lenin's *"Left-Wing" Communism, An Infantile Disorder*, we will encounter the hilarious British situation.

At the Second Congress of the Comintern in August 1920, Zinoviev (Lenin) decided to separate the hardliners from the rhetoricians; the original scenario for this project was in Lenin's *What is to be Done?* The "Twenty-One Demands" required any party in the Comintern—or one applying for membership—to meet the most rigorous standards of revolutionary dedication. Point fourteen, for example, declares, "Every party

[48]See Nettl, *op. cit.*, pp. 639, 780-781. Nettl does not confirm the charge of Lenin's direct involvement, which has been rattling around in the left-wing underground for over half a century now, but he does bring up the detail of a court of honor. Several veteran German Social Democrats have at various times told me that Pieck was in fact the finger man who disposed of Rosa Luxemburg. There is a further connection in that there is reason to believe that, at the time, the German military still considered Lenin to be an agent and that his alleged or supposed "control" happened to be the intelligence officer for the *Freikorps* unit which disposed of Rosa Luxemburg. The Social Democrat of the greatest reliability was Friedrich Stampfer who was for many years the editor of the Social Democrat paper, *Vorwärts*, was associated with the foundation of the German Republic, and was present in Berlin at the time of the Spartacus uprising.

[49]The "Twenty-one Demands," technically "conditions of admission to the Communist International approved by the Second Comintern Congress" on August 6, 1920, can be found in Degras, *op. cit.*, Vol. I, pp. 166 ff. In fact, there was a 22nd demand, which is difficult for contemporaries to understand, barring Masons. It resulted from the 19th and early 20th century notion of the Masonic International as some kind of masterful, sinister force in the world—a Trilateral Commission before its time.

[50]See Theodore Draper, *The Roots of American Communism* (New York: Viking Press, 1957), for a vivid description of the virtually Kafkaesque behavior of the left-wing of the American Socialist Party.

19

which wishes to join the Communist International [must] give unconditional support to any Soviet republic in its struggle against counterrevolutionary forces. (There had been brief Soviet republics in Hungary and Bavaria.) Communist parties must carry on unambiguous propaganda to prevent the dispatch of munitions transports to the enemies of the Soviet republics; they must also carry on propaganda by every means, legal or illegal, among the troops sent to strangle workers' republics."[51]

If this is a call for treason in the traditional sense, here is point nine, which deals with the sub-sets:

Every party which wishes to join the Communist International must carry on systematic and persistent communist activity inside the trade unions, the workers' councils and factory committees, the cooperatives, and other mass workers' organizations. Within these organizations communist cells must be organized which will by persistent and unflagging work win the trade unions, etc., for the communist cause. . . . The communist cells must be completely subordinate to the party as a whole.[52]

Point ten denounced cooperation with the "yellow Amsterdam International" of democratic trade unions and called on all parties to back the newly formed "Profintern," or Red Trade Unions International. Eventually a Peasant's International, the "Krestintern," was also established— in fact, as we shall see, by the time Willi Münzenberg finished setting up "transmission belts" for Stalin, there was an "International" for almost everything. Another central goal, brought out in point seven, was the elimination of the old Socialist leadership: Lenin wanted to bring in his own cadres. Among others listed for the chop was the American Morris "Hilquit" [sic] who, ironically, had opposed American participation in World War I.

In 1920, Lenin decided to take a direct hand in straightening out the idealists who thought the advent of the Communist International was the signal to go into business for themselves. For example, various left-wingers in Germany, who had been clobbered, year in and year out, in their efforts to gain control of the trade unions from the Social Democrats, decided to split and form pure, virginal revolutionary unions. In Britain, four or five *groupements*, including one led by the formidable Sylvia Pankhurst, were claiming sole revolutionary legitimacy.[53] They, too, thought their mission was to split the Labour Party and set up conventicles for the righteous.

---

[51]Degras, *op. cit.*, Vol. I, p. 171.

[52]*Ibid.*

[53]See Henry Pelling, *The British Communist Party* (New York: Macmillan, 1958), notably Chapter 2, "Bolshevisation 1921-4."

20

They were all in for a shock when Lenin published *"Left-Wing" Communism, An Infantile Disorder*. Essentially making a case for what was later called the "united front from below," Vladimir Ilyich told the infantile comrades to grow up. You do not split a union and march off into the wilderness singing "The International"; you stay, infiltrate, colonize, and eventually gain power. Similarly, in England, the old left-wingers who had spent their lives castigating Labour Party leaders Ramsey MacDonald and Philip Snowden for compromising with the bourgeoisie and were now looking forward to an uncompromising stance against Labour's "parliamentary fixation," were told to go hunting where the ducks were.

In other words, Lenin told the crestfallen crew of Scots Shop Stewards, Pankhurstian Women's Rights stalwarts, and idealists of the Independent Labour Party, to invade the Labour Party. Certainly, this would involve supporting "social patriots," but—in one of his favorite metaphors—this support would be analogous to the way "the rope supports the hanged man."[54] Lenin's top priority was capturing serious organizations, not running theoretical seminars on "Marxism in Our Times." The last thing he wanted was a left-wing group that, with trumpets blowing and manifestoes galore, captured itself.

Jane Degras has already compiled and edited the documents of the Third International, and those readers interested in microanalysis are referred to her magisterial three volume set.[55] What can be done here is to extract some material from the early period of the Comintern which gives specific instructions on how to fulfill Lenin's central message to the International contained in *"Left-Wing" Communism*. It might be noted that, by the Third Congress of the Comintern in June and July 1921, the early optimism about revolutionary contagion had been severely muted. "It is realized," Trotsky wrote, "that the post-war revolutionary ferment is over."[56] Lenin added that the Comintern had passed from the tactics of assault to the tactics of siege, with the objective of infiltrating the enemy camp.[57]

The Fifth Plenum of the Executive Committee of the Communist International (ECCI) set out, in May 1925, a whole series of prime targets

---

[54] *"Left-wing Communism," An Infantile Disorder* is the pure essence of Leninism. The exact quotation (urging the various British communist groups to get together and infiltrate the Labour Party) reads: "I want with my vote to support Henderson [Arthur Henderson, the leader of the Labour Party] in the same way as a rope supports a hanged man." He then goes on to denounce the "Lefts" who accuse him of lack of revolutionary virginity: "I reply to the 'Lefts' who raise this objection: don't ascribe your dogmatism to the masses!" The citation is from Lenin, *Collected Works, op. cit.*, Vol. II, p. 624.

[55] The Degras series, of which the third volume was completed in 1971, is cited in footnote 14.

[56] Cited by Degras, *op. cit.*, Vol. I, p. 224.

[57] *Ibid.*, Vol. I, p. 225.

for "Bolshevization": the trade unions, socialist parties, youth movements, women, the unemployed, and newspapers. Later in the same document, the faithful were instructed: "Besides the factory cell, and work in such organizations as trade unions, factory committees, consumers' co-operatives, etc., steps should be taken to establish a whole series of non-party subsidiary organizations—tenants' leagues, unemployed committees, ex-service men's associations, etc. [with communist cells working in them]."

Finally, "Bolshevization requires our parties to use every opportunity to make this organizational network as dense and closely woven as possible. . . . The initiative in creating such organizations must be taken by the party leadership through party members, who must then take the management of these organizations into their own hands. Communists must form fractions in these organizations, receiving instructions from the party leadership."[58] (The word "fraction" is not a typographical error for "faction." Until after World War II, Communist nuclei always referred to themselves as fractions—as, for that matter, did such heretics as the Trotskyists, Lovestoneites, Bukharinites, and others.)

In March 1926, the ECCI Plenum embroidered at some length on the techniques to be employed.[59] Though it is tedious, their document illustrates spectacularly the principle of "democratic centralism" in action, as well as Leninism's devotion to the Clausewitzian structure of military discipline. The target is a trade union, and the briefing for the cadres strongly resembles a commando unit rehearsing a covert operation:

The communist members of a trade union organization and its organs (committees, conferences, congresses, etc.) must unite into a fraction and carry on active fractional work.

The communist fractions work with all their energy to bring the majority of the trade union members under their influence.

The party executive determines the political and tactical line of the communist fractions, directs and instructs them, and controls their activity.

Candidates for all congresses, conferences, and committees shall be nominated by the fraction executive and approved by the proper party executive. If necessary, the party executive itself can nominate candidates.

The proper party executive is authorized at any time to correct or annul fraction decisions and to remove or appoint fraction executives or leaders.

---

[58]*Ibid.*, Vol. II, pp. 215-218.

[59]*Ibid.*, Vol. II, pp. 268-271. I have here used a slightly different translation from the Russian, prepared by the official Lenin Institute in Moscow, because, in the course of her editing, Degras left out several items of some interest.

In the district committees of the various trade unions, the communist members combine into a fraction.

The communist members of the central executive committee of every union shall form a fraction, which at the same time is the fraction for the entire union.

The communist fractions of the central executive committees of the various trade unions are subordinated to the communist fraction of the committee of the trade union federation. The latter shall work under the direct guidance of the Central Committee (trade union department). The CG can also deal directly with the various national fractions' executive.

Every fraction is obliged to maintain contact with the non-party oppositional elements in the trade unions. In order to make joint and unanimous action on important occasions possible, conferences and meetings must be held with these sympathizers. This applies not only to important questions of principles (international trade union unity, for or against Soviet Russia, governmental questions, etc.), but also to wage movements, factory council elections, elections on local trade union committees or trades councils, and national and international congress delegates.

The regular revenue of the party organization shall provide the means for fraction work. No special fraction dues are permitted.

These "rules of engagement"—to stick to the military metaphor—were patently designed to take control of a trade union, or of any other organization, away from its existing, probably Social Democratic, leadership by "boring from within." That is, rather than the Communists forming an alliance with the leadership of, say, the French General Confederation of Workers (CGT), they would attempt to capture the unions for their own center, the Unified Confederation of Workers (CGTU). The Comintern formulation for this was the "united front from below." This is something quite different from the "united front from above."

The first examples of the latter arose in connection with Communist policy toward the "national bourgeoisie" in colonial countries. Here the argument, made as early as the Baku Conference of the Toilers of the East in 1920 (a feature in the cinematic comedy *Reds*), was that in areas emerging from the shackles of colonialism the leaders of bourgeois anti-imperialist movements could constitute a progressive force.[60] Thus, Lenin forged a de facto alliance with Turkey's Kemal Ataturk, Indian agitators against the Raj were cultivated despite their largely upper-caste status, and Stalin carried the policy, as mentioned earlier, to the point of ordering the Chinese Communists to merge with Chiang Kai-shek's Kuomin-

---

[60]*Ibid.*, Vol. I, pp. 105-109. The recollections of the Indian, M. N. Roy, *M. N. Roy's Memoirs* (New York: Allied Publishers, 1964) are extremely interesting on this whole problem of the role of the Communist Party in the colonial areas.

tang. Indeed, Chou En-lai was the Deputy Commandant of Chiang's version of West Point, the Whampoa Military Academy!

However, in the bourgeois West (with the single exception of a brief, abortive 1923 episode in Saxony) the application of the "united front from above" tactic had to await the triumph of Hitler, and the imprimatur of the Seventh Congress of the Comintern in 1935. The only area, ironically, in which the Comintern was instructed to lie low was established when the Soviet leadership made a secret treaty with the German Army. The *Reichswehr*, barred by the Treaty of Versailles from developing advanced weapons, made them clandestinely in Russia. In return, the Soviets received a real bonus in technology transfer. A *Reichswehr* condition for this cooperation was that it be put off limits to Communist organizers![61]

This arrangement between the *Reichswehr*, virtually a state within the Weimar Republic, and Moscow has to be seen against the background of the Rapallo Treaty of 1922 in which the "two outcasts" from the European order, Germany and Soviet Russia, ended their animosity. The following year, during which the French invaded the Ruhr in response to the German default on reparations, also featured the birth of the mind-boggling Communist tactic of encouraging "National Bolshevism." The killing of a German officer by the French in the midst of riots and strikes led Karl Radek, the old Bolshevik who was in Germany trying to straighten out a Byzantine squabble in the KPD, to conceive of an alliance with furious, patriotic nationalists. Thus, for a time the "National Bolshevik" symbol was a Prussian eagle holding a hammer and sickle! This unique "united front from below" was hastily abandoned.[62] Radek, a cynical slippery type who was rumored to cheat at solitaire just to keep in form, wandered back to Moscow, became Rector of Moscow's Sun Yat-Sen University, double-crossed everybody during the consolidation of power by Stalin, was sent to Siberia during the Great Purge, and vanished.

The temptations to explore the lunatic consequences of the Sixth Comintern Congress in 1928—which led, *inter alia*, to the American Communists being told their line on the Negro problem was the establishment of a Black Republic, and the KPD being ordered into tactical alliances with the Nazis against the Social Democrats (as in the referendum to

---

[61]Gordon A. Craig, *The Politics of the Prussian Army, 1640-1945* (Oxford: Clarendon Press, 1955), pp. 409-415. See also Gerald Freund, *Unholy Alliance: Russian-German Relations from the Treaty of Brest-Litovsk to the Treaty of Berlin* (London: Chatto and Windus, 1957).

[62]Karl Radek was a singular figure who has received virtually no serious historical treatment. Probably the best short analysis of his talents is an article by Ernst Pawel, "Karl Radek—A Forgotten Pillar of Bolshevism," from *Midstream*, May 1972, pp. 33-45. On the phenomenon of national Bolshevism as a cultural aberration, see Jurgen Rühle, *Literature and Revolution* (New York: Praeger, 1969), pp. 157-160.

abolish the SPD government of Prussia)—must be resisted.[63] Suffice it to say that the election of Franklin D. Roosevelt as President of the United States in 1932 was compared by the ECCI to Mussolini's March on Rome to institute fascism.[64]

By the end of 1933, Stalin, now in absolute power, realized that Nazism was not the death-rattle of German capitalism, and began to rethink Comintern policy. Two episodes in February 1934—one in Austria, the other in France—probably triggered his shift. The first was the suppression of the Austrian Socialist Party by the Clerico-Fascists after days of bitter civil war in the workingclass sectors of Vienna. The Austrian Communists, rigidly attached to the Comintern line, took box seats to watch two wings of the degenerate bourgeoisie destroy each other. "Austro-Marxism lived in shame and died in shame," said the party's paper.[65] The Socialists went down; Hitler's troops eliminated the remnants of the right-wing Austrian regime with the 1938 *Anschluss*. However, the reactionary victors did not differentiate between the Socialists and Communists: they suppressed both with equal vigor.

During the same month in France it appeared as though a right-wing *coup d'état* was in the making. The scandal-ridden Third Republic was in the throes of *l'affaire Stavisky* which, as it unfolded, indicated widespread corruption in the legislature, the civil service, the press, and other institutions. Fascist leagues, imitating the Nazis and Mussolini's *squadristi*, mobilized to overthrow the regime. It is difficult to convey now the ferocity between those French who backed "Marianne"—*la République*—and their compatriots who called Marianne "the slut" and backed *la France*.[66]

Perhaps the symbolic point can best be made by reference to the *necrologia* in Catholic churches—religion is the ultimate ideological essence.

---

[63]Degras, *op. cit.*, Vol. II, pp. 552-557. There has been a good deal of discussion as to the origins of this concept of the Black Republic, namely, over whether it came from the American side, represented by American Negro Communists Floyd and Jones, or whether it was actually Stalin's brilliance, so to speak, in imposing the Soviet nationalities policy in the American context. Unfortunately, Theodore Draper did not analyze this particular problem in his definitive study of the American Communist party. Personal conversations with veteran black radicals indicate to me that the policy was imposed by Stalin simply on the model of his own nationalities system. For example, the late A. Philip Randolph, the distinguished black radical and trade unionist who was on the sidelines throughout this period, was convinced that the American blacks who attended the Sixth Comintern Congress felt that the policy was absurd, but that it was Stalin's and that was it. Ralph Ellison's masterful novel, *Invisible Man*, captures the flavor of this shift in the party line. Harvey Klehr's recent continuation of the Draper series through the 1930s, *The Heyday of American Communism* (New York: Basic Books, 1984), is a splendid work, but casts no further light on the provenance of the "Black Republic."

[64]Degras, *op. cit.*, Vol. III, p. 265.

[65]*Ibid.*, p. 306.

[66]For a general review of French politics in this period, see Denis W. Brogan, *France Under the Republic: The Development of Modern France (1870-1939)* (New York: Harper & Brothers, 1940).

In those areas of France controlled by the parties of the Republic—largely the industrial north, the mines, the seaports—the rubric of those appalling lists of men who died in World War I is "Died for the Republic." In the conservative, largely rural sectors, the heading reads "Died for France."

On February 6, 1934, the confrontation between the Republic and "France" (the "legal" nation and the "real" one in the phrase of the reactionary founder of *Action Française*, Charles Maurras) occurred as reactionary groups attempted to storm the Chamber of Deputies in Paris. Premier Edouard Daladier finally ordered troops to fire and the mobs were machine-gunned from the streets. Important for our purposes is that, on February 6, the French Communists (PCF) demonstrated in sympathy with the Fascists: André Marty, a long-time militant, wrote in the PCF organ *L'Humanité*, "One cannot fight against fascism without fighting against social democracy."[67] This was, of course, the French version of the KPD slogan that you could only get at the throat of capitalism over the corpse of the SPD.

However, there was movement in Moscow: Stalin was beginning to feel thoroughly isolated; the "invincible" KPD had fulfilled Lenin's caustic expectation that before German revolutionaries seized the railroads, they would buy tickets; the Japanese were on the prowl in the Far East; and now the French Republic appeared to be in dire jeopardy. The time had come to reverse gears, and France was to be the test case—particularly because while the PCF was still flirting with the *politique de pire* (the worse, the better), the French Socialists (SFIO) had launched a major initiative. On February 12, responding to the great drum last sounded in the Dreyfus crisis by Jean Jaurès, the SFIO and its trade union ally, the CGT, called a general strike in defense of the Republic.[68]

Over a million demonstrators came out in Paris, including Communists of the CGTU who, sick and tired of inane leadership, took to the streets with their Socialist comrades. This development terrified the leadership of the PCF—which, indeed, endorsed the strike the night of the eleventh to avoid being out-flanked on the left, that is, losing its militants to the SFIO because of inertia in the face of fascism. The events of February 12 convinced Stalin the time had come to move to the "united front from above" and seek a party alliance between the French Communists and Socialists.

---

[67]Cited in Val R. Lorwin, *The French Labor Movement* (Cambridge: Harvard University Press, 1954), p. 68. E. H. Carr, in his tendentious *Twilight of the Comintern* (New York: Pantheon, 1982), missed this revealing episode.

[68]*Ibid.*, pp. 68-72.

Thus, in July 1934, the PCF and SFIO signed what amounted to a treaty, a "unity of action pact" in which—while maintaining their institutional integrity—they agreed to take common steps against fascism and to protect democratic institutions.[69] In 1936, at the peak of united front sentiment (or was it "sentimentality"?), the CGT and CGTU were amalgamated into one union center which, after World War II, was captured by the Communists.[70]

---

[69]See Celie and Albert Vassart, "The Moscow Origin of the French 'Popular Front,'" in Milorad M. Drachkovitch and Branko Lazitch, editors, *The Comintern: Historical Highlights* (New York: Praeger, 1966), pp. 234-252.

[70]Lorwin, *op. cit.*

2.
Communist Operational Strategies: "Social Fascism" to Stalin's Death

"O, the Cloakmaker's Union is a no good union;
It's a company union by the bosses.
The rightwing Cloakmakers and the Socialist fakers
Are making double-crosses by the workers.
The Dubinskys, the Hillquits, and the Thomases,
Always making by the workers false promises.
They preach Socialism, but they practice fascism,
To defend capitalism by the bosses."

Song of the Communist dual union in the women's garment industry, 1928-34. The men referred to as "Labor fakers" were David Dubinsky, longtime president of the International Ladies' Garment Workers' Union, and Morris Hillquit and Norman Thomas, leading Democratic Socialists.

Although the hard-line of the Sixth Comintern Congress was *de jure* still operative, the word went out from Moscow that tentative negotiations with "social fascist" Social Democrats were in order. Even the KPD, notoriously slow on the draw, got the message in time to break ranks with the Nazis in the January 1935 Saar Plebiscite and join the local Social Democrats in calling for continued League of Nations administration instead of return to Germany.[71] (Their initial absurd, if not otherworldly, slogan had been "a Red Saar in a Red Germany"—an "objective" endorsement of the Nazi position.)

The principle of the "united front from above," later broadened to the "Popular Front," which could include non-leftist progressive elements, was carved in marble at the Seventh Congress of the Comintern in July-August 1935. The Comintern's new leader, the Bulgarian Georgi Dimitrov, recently released from a Nazi prison in exchange for a German agent caught in the Soviet Union, sounded like Thomas Jefferson. The essence of his message was that all right-minded people everywhere should rally against fascism and in defense of democratic institutions.[72] (Incidentally, Ho Chi Minh's Indochinese Communist Party was admitted to membership at this Congress.)

The Social Democrats, whose scars still ached from the social-fascist

---

[71]Degras, *op. cit.*, Vol. III, p. 342. Carr, in his *Twilight of the Comintern, op. cit.*, spends an inordinate amount of space on the shift to the Popular Front, downplaying Moscow's role.

[72]*Ibid.*, pp. 346 ff.

era, were chided—but gently—for their skepticism about the Comintern's good intentions. But the underlying theme was that, given the ominous world situation—with Italian troops in Ethiopia, Spain on the verge of exploding into civil war, Hitler obviously determined to repudiate the Treaty of Versailles and rearm, and the Japanese establishing the puppet state of Manchukuo which included areas traditionally seen as Russian spheres of influence—every effort must be made to protect and defend the "Soviet Fatherland."

The harsh positions adopted at the 1928 Comintern Congress left little room for maneuver, for creating front groups composed of left-leaning progressives or well-meaning innocents. In February 1926, under the aegis of Willi Münzenberg, a League of Oppressed Peoples was established which formally became the League Against Imperialism at its first conference in Brussels in 1927.[73] It was largely concerned with agitation in colonial areas, and in the metropoles on behalf of the oppressed, but in 1932 Münzenberg tried to broaden its base by holding in Amsterdam an international Congress Against War, featuring such Stalinist literary luminaries as Henri Barbusse and Romain Rolland.

The international Congress, in turn, was used by Münzenberg as the launching pad for various national organizations of intellectuals dedicated to the welfare and greater good of the Soviet Union. In 1933 Münzenberg's emissaries—from what he called "the Trust"—set up the first major exogenous American front group, the American League Against War and Fascism.[74] It was exogenous because the earlier groups such as the International Workers' Order, the Trade Union Unity League, or the International Labor Defense were admittedly party operations designed to achieve party goals. Its founders hoped that the League Against War and Fascism would reach out more broadly into the intellectual community; they denied Communist domination.

Until the Seventh Congress of the Comintern with its spectacular shift to the Popular Front, Willi Münzenberg's activities, while extensive, were largely limited to operations within the international Communist movement. In 1919 he had created the Communist Youth International without bothering to consult the Bolshevik cadres. This annoyed the Comintern leadership, which in 1921 ordered the group to move its headquarters to Moscow, gave Münzenberg a seat on the ECCI, and effectively incorporated the Youth International into its bailiwick.[75]

---

[73]See R. H. Carew-Hunt, "Willi Münzenberg," in D. Footman, editor, *International Communism* (London: Chatto & Windus, 1960). See also the memoir by Münzenberg's widow, Babette Gross, *Willi Münzenberg* (East Lansing, Michigan: Michigan State University Press, 1974).

[74]See I. Howe and L. Coser, *The American Communist Party* (Boston: Beacon Press, 1957), pp. 348-355.

[75]Carew-Hunt, *op. cit.*, p. 75.

Münzenberg went off to other projects, setting up the International Workers' Aid to provide food for those suffering from famine, first in the Soviet Union and later in Germany, Britain, and Japan. But his greatest achievements were in the field of political warfare and propaganda; and he set up his own financial empire, owning by the mid-twenties two German daily papers, a weekly, and a vast number of other assets. His close associate, Arthur Koestler, wrote that the "Münzenberg Trust" owned or controlled nineteen journals or magazines in Japan alone![76] He had exclusive foreign sales rights to Soviet films, and controlled publishing houses, banks, and, allegedly, bordellos as well.

In short, he had a genius for organization, but his outreach was crippled by the narrow line of the Sixth Comintern Congress: it was difficult to put together a good intellectual front, as the League Against Imperialism demonstrated, when Social Democrats were equated in the party catechism with Hitlerites. The Seventh Congress unleashed Münzenberg and his cadres. What is central to our purposes is their task: it was not to incite the workers of the world to break the chains of oppression, but to buttress the world position of the Soviet Union. Indeed, as George Orwell has chronicled in his *Homage to Catalonia*, the Spanish Communists attempted to muffle worker discontent because it would strengthen Franco's Fascists and thus work to the disadvantage of the USSR.[77]

From start to finish, the Comintern was a cynically manipulated arm of the Soviet state and its permanent cadres who were—after the idealists peeled off—utter cynics. Ignazio Silone, one of the disenchanted, told a story that provides the flavor of Comintern behavior better than fifty footnoted case studies. At a meeting of the ECCI, the topic before the conclave was how British Communists should behave when confronted by a Labour Party order that any local branch which admitted Communists be expelled.

The Russian delegate Piatnisky put forward a suggestion which seemed [obvious]. "The branches," he suggested, "should declare that they submit to the discipline demanded, and then, in practice, should do exactly the contrary."

The English Communist interrupted, "But that would be a lie." Loud laughter greeted this ingenuous objection, frank, cordial, interminable laughter the like of which the gloomy offices of the Communist International had perhaps never heard before. The joke quickly spread all over Moscow, for the Englishman's entertaining and incredible reply was telephoned at once to Stalin and the most important offices of State, provoking new waves of mirth everywhere.[78]

---

[76]Koestler, *op. cit.*, p. 253 (Danube edition).

[77](London: Faber, 1938).

[78]In Richard Crossman, editor, *The God that Failed* (New York: Harper and Brothers, 1949), p. 104.

Münzenberg was completely in this tradition: when he went about setting up fronts, he candidly called them "innocents' clubs" and "transmission belts." He shared Lenin's contempt for "useful idiots," but was always willing to utilize them to forward the objectives of the Comintern. He had a particularly supple technique with the intelligentsia, designed to service its major demand: ego caressing.

He called it "valet service," and in practice it worked as follows: No poet, however mediocre, who supported one of the party's fronts would ever lack a warm audience for a reading; fellow-traveling authors got good book reviews for works never heard of since; and, of course, political figures got the four-star treatment. Willi could fill a hall for any half-witted politician whose remarks on French-Soviet amity would always be greeted with thunderous applause. Willi loved Hollywood, not because American movies became agit-prop items, but because it was the great "milk cow." His cadres of the Hollywood Anti-Nazi League could fill the Hollywood Bowl for a benefit for Spanish Republicans, and the stars could not resist the limelight. How much of the substantial take ever reached Spain is a speculative question.

There was one overall *modus operandi:* Willi would set up a *Zentrale*, a worldwide organization, and then national affiliates would be formed. Thus, as mentioned, the World Committee Against War and Fascism spawned the American League Against War and Fascism and perhaps twenty-five other clones. Similarly, his Committee for War Relief for Republican Spain had numerous progeny.[79] Philip Toynbee, the British writer, then a young Oxford Communist, wrote in his memoir of the era that his orders from the party were "to proliferate Spanish Defense Committees throughout the university, as a moth lays its eggs in a clothes cupboard."[80] As Koestler noted, Willi produced committees as a conjurer produces rabbits out of a hat.[81]

Stalinist antics during the Popular Front era could provide the basis for a political comedy: Earl Browder proclaimed communism to be "Twentieth Century Americanism"; Maurice Thorez of the PCF offered the right hand of fellowship to the Cardinal Archbishop of Paris (and employed the familiar "tu!"); V.K. Krishna Menon suddenly abandoned Gandhi's drive for Indian freedom in unrestrained favor of the Raj; and the Spanish Communists during the Civil War denounced and then

---

[79]Carew-Hunt, *op. cit.*, p. 82.

[80]Quoted in Hugh Thomas, *The Spanish Civil War* (London: Eyre and Spottiswoode, 1961), p. 305.

[81]Koestler, *op. cit.*, p. 254. A fine study of *Interlocking Subversion in Government Departments*, issued in 1953 by the Senate Judiciary Committee (83rd Congress, 1st Session), indicates this technique was utilized for more than propaganda purposes.

31

murdered "radical" disrupters on the left who demanded land reform and other measures that might frighten the bourgeois parties.[82]

Far more important, however, was the extent to which the Popular Front line established the Stalinists as the leading anti-Nazis. In September 1934, prefiguring the shift in Comintern policy, the Soviet Union joined the League of Nations, traditionally denounced as a "den of thieves," and its eloquent representative, Maxim Litvinov, day in, day out, called for "collective security" against the Fascist powers. This was at a time when the Western powers were engaged in "appeasement" (a word which only later became pejorative) in the interests of peace.

With the Soviet Union seemingly in the front rank of those defending freedom against the Fascists, it became extremely bad form to discuss internal events in Stalin's fiefdom, where the paroxysm of the Great Purges was in full force. It must have strained the credulity of Western progressives to learn that virtually all of Lenin's comrades in arms had been British, French, Japanese, or American (or any combination of the above) spies whom the vigilant Stalin had unmasked. But there were the "Confessions," and why would Zinoviev say what he said about his wicked past if it were not true? As far as the behavior of the progressive Western intelligentsia when faced with these patent fantasies is concerned, the less said the better.

A number of Comintern insiders, who knew the cast of characters intimately, tried to distance themselves from the bloodbath, but Willi Münzenberg, a leading case in point, could not bring himself to a public denunciation of the trials. This would have made him an "objective pro-Hitlerite" because he would have been undermining the reputation of Stalin, the leader in the fight against Nazism. But whether Münzenberg and others like him went public or not was of little interest to the secret police: as potential witnesses against the great Stalin, they were on the OGPU's liquidation list. Those interested in details are referred to Robert Conquest's definitive study, *The Great Terror*.[83] (Although the Soviet secret police changed its acronym from OGPU to NKVD and subsequently to KGB, I have used the former.)

Thus, in a somber historical paradox, just at the time Stalin and his butchers were killing, or shipping to certain Gulag deaths, some fifteen million people, the standing of the Soviet Union as a defender of the peace and as a bulwark of anti-Nazism in the Spanish Republic reached its apex in the West. The innocents accepted the bona fides of Soviet

---

[82]See Bolloten, *op. cit.*

[83](New York: Macmillan Co., 1968).

justice, as incorporated in Stalin's model Constitution of 1936, while the more sophisticated agreed that a mistake may have been made here and there, but to make an omelette you have to break eggs. Stalin himself noted that the death of one person is a tragedy; of a million, a statistic.

Meanwhile, Hitler was on the move, reoccupying the Rhineland, seizing Austria, and increasing demands on Czechoslovakia and Poland. German planes and Italian troops were fighting with Franco's rebels against the forces of the Spanish Republic. The West, in contrast, was inert: the United States, autarkic and autistic, might as well have been on the moon. We were wholly wrapped up in the economic problems of the Great Depression, were convinced we had been tricked into World War I by "merchants of death" and British intelligence, and not only boycotted the League of Nations from the outset, but refused to join the World Court in 1935.

Britain and France were dominated by an elite, the survivors of the generation of 1914 who were, with a handful of exceptions, convinced that war was *the* ultimate disaster and that any steps to forestall armed conflict were justified. This led to an orgy of collective auto-hypnosis in which "Herr Hitler" and "Signor Mussolini" were treated as rational players on the diplomatic chess board who, if properly understood, could be persuaded to abandon their dreams of aggression. It was the leader of the British Labour Party, George Lansbury, who in 1938 reported that when he interviewed Hitler, "I looked deeply into his eyes and was convinced of the man's sincerity when he said he desired peace most of all."[84]

On the other side of the British political fence, Conservative Prime Minister Stanley Baldwin in 1936 confessed his reasons for opposing rearmament in the 1935 General Election: "Supposing I had gone to the country and said that Germany was rearming, and that we must rearm, does anybody think this peaceful democracy would have rallied to that cause at that moment? I cannot think of anything that would have made the loss of the election from my point of view more certain."[85]

In 1935, in a masterstroke of political warfare, Hitler signed the Anglo-German Naval Treaty, promising to keep the *Reich's* navy at one-third of British strength. This further inflamed British-French relations: French leaders were convinced "perfidious Albion" was going to make a deal

---

[84]A relic of this attitude, which was splendidly described in A. L. Rowse's *All Souls and Appeasement* (London: Macmillan, 1961), is A. J. P. Taylor's *The Origins of the Second World War* (New York: Atheneum, 1961). On Lansbury, see Raymond Postgate, *The Life of George Lansbury* (London: Longmans, 1951), pp. 313-315.

[85]Cited by R. V. Jones in *1945-1979: Victory into Defeat?*, published lecture to the Standing Conference of Employers of Graduates at York University, July 5, 1979.

behind their backs with Germany. And it proved to be a self-inflicted wound: As British intelligence reported consistent Nazi violations of the treaty (e.g., the building of "pocket-battleships"), the government suppressed the revelations. To admit it had been duped was unthinkable; besides, if the admission were made that Hitler was cheating, something might have to be done about it. (The reception given President Reagan's January 1984 report on Soviet treaty violations obviously gave some of us a decided sense of *deja vu*.)

In France the situation was, if possible, worse. The abattoir of World War I was still fresh in the memories of politicians and ordinary people—even in an era dominated by the possibilities of nuclear destruction, we are stunned by the lists of World War I dead on French battle monuments. Thus, Hitler was permitted to reoccupy the Rhineland without the slightest French resistance, although his generals had been instructed to withdraw in the event of any hostile response. As in Britain, the Socialists—led by the Popular Front Premier Léon Blum—combined verbal anti-fascism with anti-militarism.[86]

The Munich Interlude

The background and events at Munich have been explored *ad infinitum* elsewhere. What is important for our purposes is the impact on the Communist world of the September 29, 1938 pact between Britain, France, Germany, and Italy. The Soviet Union had been excluded from the discussions, and a less suspicious man than Stalin could have read the proceedings and discerned a coalition against the USSR. Much has been made by some revisionist historians of a purported Soviet willingness to fight the fascists in defense of Czechoslovakia. Noises to that effect did later emerge from Moscow, but, in fact, by 1937 Stalin had shot his top generals (superbly framed by Himmler's Gestapo) and 80 percent of his officer corps, resulting in military leadership problems that were not overcome until roughly 1943.

No, Stalin did not call for his horse: he began shifting his course to turn the obviously impending Nazi assault west against Britain and France. Shortly after Munich, on the anniversary of the Soviet Revolution, the Comintern issued a remarkably aesopian manifesto announcing "the second imperialist war has already begun . . . a war for a new partition of the world . . . the imperialist cliques of England and France have signed a counter-revolutionary alliance with German and Italian fas-

---

[86]See Nathaniel Greene, *Crisis and Decline: The French Socialist Party in the Popular Front Era* (Ithaca, N.Y.: Cornell University Press, 1969).

34

cism."[87] This was tenuously attached to the Popular Front policy by calling on the people of Britain and France to turn out the appeasers in power.

Stalin, however, knew that—to their surprise—British Prime Minister Neville Chamberlain and French Premier Edouard Daladier had been greeted as saviors on returning from Munich. As the influential E. H. Carr noted in the first edition of *The Twenty Years Crisis* (1939), "The negotiations which led up to the Munich Agreement . . . were the nearest approach in recent years to the settlement of a major international issue by a procedure of peaceful change." In short, Stalin, who was already fighting a massive, undeclared war with Japan, featuring, *inter alia*, tank battles on the Soviet-Manchurian border, interpreted Munich as an invitation to Hitler to go east and confront the USSR with a two-front war—a logistical nightmare as the fronts were some 5,000 miles apart.

If the Munich Pact had been designed with such Machiavellian calibration, it would have been a masterpiece of *realpolitik*. The difficulty is that all the evidence indicates that the leading Western participants were simply engaged in desperate improvisation to forestall the ultimate horror of war. Without question, there were those in France and Germany who hoped Munich would lead to a German attack on Russia, but their input into the policymaking process has never been documented.

Moreover, had the French and British carefully devised this scheme, would they, after Hitler occupied the remnants of Czechoslovakia on March 15, 1939, have locked themselves into a military treaty on March 31 and April 6 to guarantee the integrity of Poland? In Britain and France the same men who had destroyed the eminently defensible Czechoslovakia (as relieved *Wehrmacht* officers confirmed when they later peacefully inspected the formidable Sudetenland defenses) rushed six months later to guarantee utterly indefensible Poland.

But Stalin was not the type who understood the elemental rage of honorable men who suddenly realized the extent of Hitler's duplicity and their responsibility for the disaster. The Polish guarantee was a political id-discharge, an emotional spasm, taken without the slightest concern for the military situation on the ground. Then somebody looked at a map and reached the obvious conclusion: the time had come to form an alliance with Stalin.

To make a long story short, throughout the summer of 1939 a Western mission tried to reach terms with the Soviets, but they were caught in a trap: Stalin's preconditions for any alliance, pared of ambiguous rhetoric, were the annexation of Estonia, Latvia, Lithuania, and Bessarabia, and hegemony over Poland. Giving Poland to Moscow—the inexorable con-

---

[87]Degras, *op. cit.*, Vol. III, p. 443.

sequence of Stalin's demand that Soviet troops operate freely in Poland—
was hardly a way of defending Polish integrity. And had the British and
French leaders told their parliaments that they had just donated the
Baltic States to Russia as a good-will offering, they would probably have
been lynched.

The Soviets, however, were simply playing cat and mouse games. As
early as February 1937, a message had been sent from Moscow to Berlin
by a back channel—Kandelaki, a Soviet "trade envoy" who was also a
member of Stalin's personal secretariat—that Britain and France were
unreliable and that nothing would please the Soviet people more than a
rapprochement with their German friends.[88] This approach stalled, but
in April 1939 Walter Krivitsky, a top OGPU officer in Western Europe
before defecting to the United States in 1937, predicted the Stalin-Hitler
Pact in the *Saturday Evening Post*.[89]

Krivitsky was denounced and possibly murdered ("suicided" was the
word invented for the occasion), but in the summer of 1939 the Moscow-
Berlin courtship moved into high gear: on August 20 a trade pact was
concluded, and on the 23rd Nazi Foreign Minister von Ribbentrop arrived
in Moscow to sign a Treaty of Non-Aggression.

Warmly entertained by Stalin and Foreign Commissar V. M. Molotov,
Ribbentrop gave the Baltic States, over half of Poland, and the Rumanian
province of Bessarabia to the USSR "in the event of a political and
territorial rearrangement," an aesopian phrase for the forthcoming attack
by the *Wehrmacht* on Poland, which was launched on schedule September
1. On September third, Britain and France fulfilled the terms of their
Polish commitment and declared war on Germany.

Were it not for its tragic dimensions, the reaction of the world Communist movement to the Nazi-Soviet Pact could best be compared to a
drunken square dance. Indeed, the Executive Committee of the Comintern seemed to be in a coma until November. The central question
once war had broken out was the attitude of the Western Communist
parties toward their governments' participation. To put it another way,
did Stalin's deal with Hitler interfere with, say, the French Communist
Deputies' support for the French war effort? Or, was the Nazi-Soviet
Pact a bond which required Communists everywhere to be "objectively"
pro-Nazi by opposing rearmament, conscription, and military appropriations?

The auguries initially were cryptic. At the Moscow banquet celebrating

---

[88]Cited in John Erickson, *The Soviet High Command* (New York: St. Martin's, 1962), pp. 396-397, 432,
453, 458, 464.

[89]Issue of April 29, 1939.

the signature of the Pact, Stalin toasted Hitler: "I know how much the German nation loves its Fuehrer; I therefore wish to drink to his health." Yet Stalin was the father of what Orwell called "newspeak," the use of words to convey the opposite of their meaning. Thus the assertion that the German people loved Hitler could be interpreted as a limiting statement. The Nazis present took the toast (correctly) at face value and obviously got along famously with their Communist hosts. Ribbentrop later reported that at the festivities he felt as though he were in the company of old Nazi comrades.[90] Hitler reciprocated by telling his top generals on August 22 that "Stalin and I, we are alone in foretelling the future."[91]

But what about the poor French, British, German, American, and other Communists who were suddenly confronted with the unthinkable? Let us look at a few examples: First, the PCF whose *doyen* Marcel Cachin wrote the Socialist Leon Blum, "The Communist Party of France affirms that, should Hitler declare war on France, he will have against him the entire French people, with the Communists in the front rank ... [we] will do nothing to hamper the unity so indispensable for the defense of the country."[92] PCF Deputies voted for total mobilization and war appropriations, and promised to be "the best defenders of democracy and the independence of France."[93] Twenty-one Communist Deputies out of 72 resigned in disgust at the pact.

The German KPD, in exile, went through the tortures of the damned—there were a number of suicides—but on August 25 their Central Committee welcomed the Pact as "a step towards peace," but urged the German people to continue the fight against Nazism. The KPD concluded that if Hitler went to war, "every German must realize that national-socialism is guilty of the war."[94]

The British Communist leader Harry Pollitt similarly decoupled Stalin's policy toward Hitler from the objectives of the Communist movement in his book entitled *How to Win the War*. The logic was convoluted. The British Communist argued that the Pact had eased matters for Britain and France: "It sets free their forces and thereby enables them better to resist the aggressor in Europe." In the event of war, wrote another leading cadre, J. R. Campbell, "the British people must fight to secure the over-

---

[90]Cited in A. Rossi (pseud.: A. Tasca), *Deux ans d'alliance Germano-Sovietique* (Paris: Librairie Arthéme Fayard, 1949), p. 85.

[91]*Ibid.*, p. 88.

[92]Degras, *op. cit.*, Vol. III, p. 439.

[93]*Ibid.*

[94]*Ibid.*

whelming defeat of fascism."[95] When their position was understandably give the acid treatment, the British Communists announced with aplomb that, in fact, Russia had saved the Poles from the Nazis.[96]

The American Communists, long considered the village idiots of the Comintern, put on a spectacular exhibition of political Dada: the *Daily Worker* did not mention the pact for twenty-four hours. Then, General Secretary Earl Browder made the gnomic pronouncement that every country should sign a non-aggression pact with the Soviet Union, that it was a "masterstroke for peace."[97] Subsequently, the *Daily Worker* discerned the true meaning of the coalition: it was "a smashing blow at Munich treachery. . . . By *compelling Germany to sign* a non-aggression pact, the Soviet Union has tremendously limited the direction of Nazi war aims."[98]

The absence of any clarification from Moscow for almost two months can only be understood as a reflection of Stalin's overall contempt for the Comintern, which he once described in a Russian slang term, "little store," variously translated as "gyp-joint" or "thieves-kitchen." Also, of course, the technical boss of the Comintern, Georgi Dimitrov, was not going to move without instructions from Stalin—that was a high-risk enterprise—and the Soviet leader was too busily engaged in the real estate business, taking over the Baltic States and Poland, in the fall of 1939 to worry about the psychic burdens of such as Earl Browder or Harry Pollitt.

We will resist an inch-by-inch walk through this period and simply note that, by November, and thanks to the ECCI Resolution issued on the anniversary of the Soviet Revolution, the international party line was set in concrete: Britain and France were the guilty parties in launching the "Second Imperialist War."[99] (Earl Browder, to make up for his previous slowness off the post, wrote a book with that title which, unfortunately, was published before the Nazi invasion of Russia wholly altered the "correlation of forces.")

Once the Nazi-Soviet Pact was perceived not merely as a tactical ruse on Stalin's part, much of the support the Communists had gained for their leading anti-fascist role vanished overnight: duped idealists and fellow-travelers deserted *en masse*. But the hard-core shifted gears and initiated anti-war campaigns in the democracies, including efforts by

---

[95]*Ibid.*

[96]*Ibid.*, p. 441.

[97]Howe and Coser, *op. cit.*, p. 387.

[98]*Ibid.* (Italics added.)

[99]Degras, *op. cit.*, Vol. III, p. 443.

38

Communist-dominated trade unions in the United States to block the production of military equipment.[100]

In the United States, the most effective "front," one of Willi Münzenberg's children, the American League for Peace and Democracy (*né* The American League against War and Fascism) met in Chicago, rebaptized itself The American Peace Mobilization, and adopted the credo "The Yanks are Not Coming!"[101] In India, V. K. Krishna Menon, last heard of as a militant pro-British spokesman against fascism and opponent of the Indian independence movement, demanded instant action against the British imperialists.

And so it went throughout the world with the PCF actually asking the German Military Governor of occupied Paris for permission to publish *l'Humanité*.[102] PCF leader Maurice Thorez deserted from the army and urged all lovers of true freedom to do likewise. Probably the most odious incident was the private treaty between the OGPU and the Gestapo to exchange prisoners: the OGPU gave the Nazis a number of German Communists in return for Communist agents imprisoned in Germany.[103]

We have already examined Stalin's indifference to warnings that the *Wehrmacht* had "Operation Barbarossa" on the drawing boards. Once it was clear to Hitler that "Operation Sealion," the invasion of Britain, was not a wise option, preparation for invading Russia went into high gear. On June 22, 1941, the huge German barrage opened up and the blitz began, rolling up the wholly unready Soviet forces like a rug.

The surprise of the Soviet high command was equaled only by the bafflement of the international Communist movement: switching sides and the rhetoric necessary to justify reversal of positions were getting to be a bit overpowering. My favorite memory of that period was a man carrying a hand-made sign hastily altered from "The Yanks are Not Coming!" to "The Yanks are Not Coming Too Late!"

For once the American Communist Party was not caught off base, but was in safe by a whisker. Philip J. Jaffe, longtime confidant of Earl Browder, relates that on the weekend of June 22, 1941, "I attended and participated in a lecture session on foreign affairs at a camp in upstate New York. Among those present was the entire editorial board of the Communist weekly magazine, the *New Masses!*" It happened that the forthcoming issue of the *New Masses* denouncing Roosevelt and Churchill

---

[100]Howe and Coser, *op. cit.*, pp. 397-398.

[101]See Philip Jaffe, *The Rise and Fall of American Communism* (New York: Horizon Press, 1975), p. 47.

[102]Cited in A. Rossi (pseud.: A. Tasca), *Les Communistes Français pendant la Drôle de Guerre* (Paris: Les Iles D'Or, 1951), pp. 324 ff.

[103]See Margaret Buber-Neumann, *Under Two Dictators* (London: Gollancz, 1949).

as warmongers was about to go to press. The editors "hurried back to New York to rewrite it. The revised edition appeared in time, and in it Hitler became the warmonger and Roosevelt . . . once again became the peace-loving democrat."[104]

The Comintern did not bother to issue any statement revising the "general line": it was obvious. Overnight, Communists in all Western countries became superpatriots, and Communists and fellow-travelers in colonial areas were told to cooperate with their recent oppressors, rather than to continue their anti-imperialist campaigns. Their main slogans became "Defend the Soviet Union!" and "A Second Front Now!" With the *Wehrmacht* at the gates of Moscow by Christmas 1941, the demand for an immediate Allied attack on the Nazi rear was heard at an increasing pitch. A major effort in the summer and fall of 1941 was to get the United States into the war, an orchestration which ended on December 11, 1941, when Hitler, in a moment of geopolitical insanity, and under no treaty obligation with Japan to do so, declared war on us. However, the military strength of the United States in 1941 was latent, not actual: there were barely two million men in the armed forces, mostly raw, untrained draftees—the 1940 figure was less than half a million!—and the total military budget amounted to just over six billion dollars.[105] The United States, in short, was a giant without a shadow.

Even when American lend-lease was a vital component of Soviet resistance, Stalin proved a most uncooperative ally; yet President Franklin D. Roosevelt convinced himself that, if treated properly, "Uncle Joe" would become a well-behaved member of the world community.[106] FDR—who was never immodest about his personal powers of persuasion—decided to launch what is now called "summitry," gathering together Churchill, Stalin, and himself to work out the problems of the world.

The conference took place in Teheran, Iran, in November 1943, and Roosevelt devised an elaborate game-plan to alleviate Stalin's anxieties about Western intentions. Fundamentally, it was based on the premise that Stalin was paranoid about an Anglo-American conspiracy against him. Certainly in the case of Churchill there was a substantial historical basis for Soviet suspicion: in 1919 Winston had urged that Bolshevism be "strangled in its cradle."[107]

---

[104]Jaffe, *op. cit.*, p. 49.

[105]*Historical Statistics of the United States: Colonial Times to 1970* (Washington: Bureau of the Census, 1975), Vol. II, pp. 1141, 1116.

[106]See, for a detailed description, John R. Deane, *The Strange Alliance* (New York: Viking, 1947). For a sourly humorous episode, see R. V. Jones, *The Wizard War* (New York: Coward, McCann & Geoghegan, 1978), pp. 441-442.

[107]See R. Ullman, *Britain and the Russian Civil War* (Princeton, N.J.: Princeton University Press, 1968), pp. 90-98.

Thus Roosevelt began to court Stalin, attempting to convince the hardened *apparatchik* that he, FDR, had reservations about Churchill and the British Empire. According to Frances Perkins, to whom he delightedly told the story, he "began to tease Churchill about his Britishness, about John Bull, about his cigars, about his habits. It began to register with Stalin. Winston got red and scowled and the more he did so, the more Stalin smiled. Finally, Stalin broke out into a deep, heavy guffaw, and for the first time in three days I saw light . . . it was then I called him 'Uncle Joe' . . . from that time on our relations were personal . . . the ice was broken and we talked like men and brothers."[108] One wishes Stalin's version of this ingenuous ploy were on the record; one suspects he told Molotov, "That Roosevelt's a simpleton—I could eat him for breakfast."

Stalin did go home happy. He received a hard commitment to the Second Front in the summer of 1944, while stonewalling on the liberation of the Baltic states, on postwar Poland, and on every other issue of consequence. Some of this "Spirit of Teheran" must have been transmitted in Communist circles, for as "Commissars" became "Ministers," the "International" was replaced as the Soviet anthem, and the Comintern was formally abolished, it seemed to some cadres that Stalin had abandoned the traditional rigidity of the worldwide apparat. At least this was the message Earl Browder received, and it led him to write the pamphlet *Teheran and America* which emphasized that "capitalism and socialism have begun to find a way to peaceful coexistence and collaboration in the same world." He was particularly impressed by the dismantling of the Comintern.

The crux of the matter lay in Browder's endorsement of FDR for President in 1944 and his promise that the Communists "frankly declare that we are ready to cooperate in making capitalism work effectively in the post-war period with the least possible burden upon the people!"[109] As Jaffe points out, this pamphlet was widely circulated in many languages throughout Western Europe—it was even translated into Indonesian—and summarized in *Inprecorr* (International Press Correspondence, a Comintern newsletter which continued to appear under the auspices of the "ghost Comintern"). In April 1944, he received warm praise from André Marty, the French Communist, who had graduated from being a Stalinist hangman in the Spanish Civil War to membership in the Provisional Cabinet of Charles de Gaulle's French government in Algiers.[110] (A junior member of this government once told me De Gaulle—

---

[108]Cited in James MacGregor Burns, *Roosevelt: The Soldier of Freedom 1940-1945* (New York: Harcourt, Brace, Jovanovich, 1970), p. 412.

[109]Jaffe, *op. cit.*, p. 55.

[110]*Ibid.*

on whom Marty had been forced by Anglo-American pressure—used to focus on the Communist's thick neck, as if visualizing where the guillotine should hit!)

With all lights apparently green, Browder proceeded to take his thesis to its logical conclusion: the two-party system in the United States provided "adequate channels for the basic democratic rights."[111] The Communist Party U.S.A. was therefore superfluous and should transform itself essentially into an interest group. The well-drilled comrades, assuming the command of Browder was the will of Moscow, did a disciplined "To the rear, march!" At its 1944 Convention, the Party immolated itself and rose from the ashes as the Communist Political Association, a "nonparty organization of Americans, which, basing itself on the working class, carries forward the traditions of Washington, Jefferson, Paine, Jackson, and Lincoln. . . ."[112]

The short, happy life of the Communist Political Association merits examination in depth because its demise symbolized a worldwide change in the "general line" from wartime fraternity between the Soviet Union and the West to a renewal of hostility in the Cold War. By the spring of 1945, the Germans were on the verge of surrender—it occurred on May 7—and Stalin, abetted by his top aide Andrei Zhdanov, decided to call off the comradely charade. His technique was, to say the least, bizarre: on May 22, 1945, readers of the *New York World Telegram* were treated to a feature story by Frederick Woltman about an article by French Communist Jacques Duclos (known in PCF circles as *l'oeil de Moscou*) in the April 1945 issue of the PCF *Cahiers du Communisme*.[113]

Woltman was generally considered a prize "red baiter" in left-wing circles and was not a likely subscriber to a French Communist theoretical journal, but there was his story on Duclos' denunciation of "Browderism," "On the Dissolution of the Communist Party of the U.S.A." It was a wideranging assault on Browder's interpretation of the Spirit of Teheran for its failure to recognize the implacable, fundamental hostility between communism and capitalism. In particular, Duclos excoriated the American's heretical assumption that "the greatest part of Europe, west of the Soviet Union, will probably be reconstituted on a bourgeois-democratic basis and not on a fascist-capitalist or Soviet basis."[114]

"In truth," Duclos concluded, "nothing justifies the dissolution of the American Communist Party," an act based on the false premise "of a long

[111]*Ibid.*, p. 66.

[112]*Ibid.*, p. 67.

[113]*Ibid.*, p. 68.

[114]John R. Roche, "Life Among the Stalinists," *The New Leader*, May 17, 1982, p. 9.

peace between the classes in the United States, the possibility of suppressing class warfare in the post-war period, and the establishment of harmony between labor and capital."[115] Implicit in Duclos' critique was the Zhdanov thesis that the United States and other Western countries would suffer a profound economic crisis in the wake of the war, a crisis which Communists should be prepared to capitalize upon in their quest for power.

Although Browder was unaware of it, his political death warrant was written in an internal Soviet dispute over the future of capitalism in which the principal figure in opposition to the Zhdanov faction was the economist Eugen Varga, who denied that capitalism was on the ropes because wartime experience had involved extensive utilization of state planning. That story is beyond our concern here, except to note that Andrei Zhdanov was the Stalinist "point-man" in the USSR's postwar suppression of independence in Eastern Europe, the founder of the Cominform, and Stalin's heir-apparent—until he overplayed his hand and was probably executed.[116]

To return to Woltman's remarkable scoop, the interesting question is: Who gave him the *Cahiers* and translated the Duclos article? This was as neat a sandbagging as one could imagine. According to his account, Woltman had a call from a diplomat who happened to be a Ukrainian delegate to the United Nations founding conference then laboring in San Francisco. The Communist emissary sent him an envelope containing the translated Duclos article, and said "You may find this interesting."[117] For some reason he did not drop off a copy for his comrades at the *Daily Worker*.

The initial American Communist reaction was catatonic. The first line was that the article was a fake, an imperialist trick, but two days after Woltman's article appeared, the *Daily Worker* ran the piece and the National Board of the Communist Political Association went into continuous session. To make a squalid story short, William Z. Foster, Browder's ancient rival for the leadership of the Communist movement, who had complained about abolishing the Party but had not openly opposed it, mobilized all the top cadres at a Pentecostal rally on July 26, 1945. Browder was removed as President of the Communist Political Association and the Communist Party was reconstituted. Six months later Browder was formally expelled from the CPUSA.[118]

---

[115]*Ibid.*

[116]See Gavriel Ra'anan, *International Policy Formulation in the U.S.S.R.: Factional "Debates" during the Zhdanovshchina* (New York: Archon Books, 1983).

[117]Conversations with Woltman, 1946-47.

[118]Jaffe, *op. cit.*, p. 82.

The "Return to Normalcy"

The purge of Browder and repudiation of the Browder "class-collaboration" thesis was a harbinger of the new hard general line that was firming up in Moscow as the war moved to a successful conclusion. On February 9, 1946, Stalin delivered an "election speech"—there was an election to the Supreme Soviet scheduled for the 10th for which Stalin, presumably, was nervously campaigning. In this speech he set up the barricade between the socialist way and the capitalist route to economic catastrophe. He downplayed the role of the British and Americans in winning the war and asserted "the Soviet social system is a truly popular system, issued from the depths of the people and enjoying its mighty support" equipped with a "first-class modern army with completely up-to-date armament, most experienced commanders and high morale and combat qualities."[119]

There are two schools of thought on what triggered this stark break with the "Spirit of Teheran": First, that the Americans in some way or other—the "revisionist" historians disagree among themselves on the provocation—had made it clear to the Soviets that the era of cooperation was to be replaced by a return to the hostility of the past, that the impending "Third Crisis in World Capitalism" mandated the destruction of the socialist enemy.[120] The second explanation, to me persuasive, downgrades the role of the West in favor of an intricate power struggle within the Soviet bureaucracy between the followers of Zhdanov, then ascendant, and Malenkov.[121]

However interesting this dispute may be, space considerations require it be left to Sovietologists. Whatever the cause, the objective consequence was a worldwide declaration of hostilities, later dubbed the "Cold War," which saw the Stalinists creating the Cominform in 1947 to consolidate Eastern Europe and repudiate the "Semi-Browderism" of the French

---

[119]*New York Times*, February 19, 1946.

[120]Suffice it to say that I look on the "revisionist historians" of the origins of the Cold War in roughly the same fashion an astrophysicist views the flat-worlders. For a devastating and conclusive analysis of their bizarre "research," see Robert J. Maddox, *The New Left and the Origins of the Cold War* (Princeton, N.J.: Princeton University Press, 1973).

[121]The extent to which Soviet foreign policy can be a virtually accidental spinoff from internal feuds in the Stalinist bureaucracy was first emphasized by Boris I. Nicolaevsky, who sometimes seemed uncanny. I recall his prediction in the *New Leader* of a Nazi-Soviet rapprochement in the spring of 1939 (like Krivitsky) on the basis of a speech by Stalin to the 18th Party Congress. Similarly, another old Menshevik roared, "Poor Maxim [Litvinov] will soon be hammered!" (See my "Remembering the Levitas Salon," *New Leader*, December 15, 1980.) The pun here is that Molotov, who indeed replaced Litvinov as Foreign Commissar on May 3, 1939, means hammer in Russian. For a selection of Nicolaevsky's microanalyses, see *Power and the Soviet Elite* (New York: Praeger, 1965). A superb application of this technique to the period under discussion is Gavriel Ra'anan's study of the *Zhdanovshchina, op. cit., passim.*

44

and Italian Communist parties which were then participating in the governments of those nations.

Elsewhere, notably in Asia after the 1947 Calcutta Congress of the World Federation of Democratic Youth—a major "transmission belt"—abortive insurrections were launched in Burma, Malaya, and Indonesia, and the Indian Communist Party opted for revolutionary violence against the newly independent Nehru Government.[122] There was even a futile and largely unnoticed mini-putsch in Chile.[123]

On the big stage, the new hard line was dedicated to the frustration of American efforts to protect Greece and Turkey and rebuild the economies of Western Europe. Although Stalin was accused of having designs on the world—and perhaps he did have an occasional hubristic dream—his fundamental policy can be described as strategically defensive, tactically offensive. But he was extremely cautious and anything but overwhelmed by the potency of Marxism-Leninism as an election manifesto. When Djilas asked him why the Communists had not succeeded in France and Italy, his reply was "No Red Army."[124]

Indeed, there is good reason to believe that most of the adventuristic forays described above—Greece, Burma, Malaya, Indonesia, Chile—were put in train when Zhdanov and his allies, Georgi Dmitrov and the Titoists, were in the saddle and Stalin was largely *hors de combat* with a heart ailment.[125] Stalin always looked on Greece and Yugoslavia as marginal states in the zone between British and Soviet spheres of influence. (Knowledge of this probably influenced Tito and Djilas in 1943 when they offered to fight alongside the Nazis in the event of a British invasion of Dalmatia.[126])

The Communist insurrection in Greece in late 1944 against the British and what was formerly the Greek government-in-exile was clearly a Titoist initiative. The intermittent civil war which raged for the next four

---

[122]See Frank N. Trager, editor, *Marxism in Southeast Asia* (Stanford, Calif.: Stanford University Press, 1949), pp. 263-266. After Trager's book was published, conclusive evidence of the Yugoslav influence in Calcutta was published by the Indian Communist Party in its "July, 1950 Report on Leftwing Sectarianism," cited by Ra'anan, *op. cit.*, pp. 111-115.

[123]Ra'anan, *op. cit.*, p. 114.

[124]This prefigured a later war of words on Tito's claim that the Partisans, not the Red Army, liberated Yugoslavia. Moscow's retort was that communist governments existed only under the auspices of the Red Army. See Mosa Pijade, *La Fable de l'aide Sovietique à l'Insurrection Nationale Yougoslave* (Paris: Le Livre Yougoslave, 1950), for the authorized Titoist version.

[125]See Ra'anan, *op. cit.*, pp. 179-180.

[126]See Walter R. Roberts, *Tito, Mihailovic and the Allies, 1941-1945* (New Brunswick, N.J.: Rutgers University Press, 1973), pp. 108-112. For further detail on the negotiations between the Nazis and the three top Titoists, Djilas, Velobit, and Popovic—including Djilas' later justification of the attempted deal, see David Martin, editor, *Patriot or Traitor: The Case of General Mihailovich* (Stanford, Calif.: Hoover Institution, 1978), pp. 44-45.

years was mounted from Yugoslavia and Bulgaria—Zhdanovite strong-
holds—and collapsed in 1948 when Stalin had the Yugoslavs expelled
from the Cominform. Dmitrov died in Moscow, possibly a natural death,
and the Greek Communist leader Markos sought sanctuary in the USSR.
In 1948 Zhdanov died as natural a death as did Dmitrov—at least the
same five doctors signed the death certificates.[127]

While the grounds for expelling Tito from the Cominform were somewhat exotic in substance—he and Dmitrov had worked out a plan for a
Balkan Federation which would have included Bulgaria and Yugoslavia
and fostered "Macedonian unity"—the essential reason was that Stalin,
health regained, decided to close the Zhdanovite playground.[128] If one
recalls that the occasion for American reappraisal of its postwar options
was the Greek Civil War and Soviet territorial demands on Turkey (which
led to the formulation of the Truman Doctrine on March 12, 1947), there
was every reason for Stalin to denounce the "adventurers" who had
roused the sleeping giant. Suddenly the Titoists, who had been more
Stalinist than Stalin, were sentenced to death *in absentia* for heresy.

With the one significant exception of the durability of the Nazi-Soviet
Pact, Stalin was a realist. Thus, no matter what Zhdanov's kept economist,
N. A. Voznesenskii, might say about the imminent collapse of American
capitalism, Stalin had witnessed the U.S. economy go from a cold start
in 1940-41 to the "Arsenal of Democracy" in 1944-45.[129] In fact, one
could argue that the extreme course taken by the Zhdanovites had pro-
voked a war crisis in the United States which would undermine Voznesenskii's thesis by fueling the economy. However motivated, Stalin shot
both Voznesenskii and the latter's brother, the Zhdanovite Leningrad
leader.[130]

For Stalin the *mot d'ordre* became the consolidation of the Soviet sphere
and the subversion of a strong Western Europe which would include
Germany. He was frustrated in his efforts to retake Yugoslavia—Tito
and Djilas had learned the survival drill under a hard master.

One anomaly remained: Czechoslovakia. Although today we seem to
take for granted Czechoslovakia's status as part of the Soviet sphere in
Eastern Europe, in 1945 the state created by Thomas Masaryk in 1918
was considered part of the "West." Indeed, in 1945 President Eduard

---

[127]Robert Conquest, *Power and Policy in the USSR* (New York: Harper, 1967), pp. 163-165.

[128]See Stephen E. Palmer, Jr., and Robert R. King, *Yugoslav Communism and the Macedonian Question* (Hamden, Conn., Archon, 1971).

[129]See N.A. Voznesenskii, *The Economy of the USSR during World War II* (Washington: Public Affairs Press, 1948).

[130]See Leonard Schapiro, *The Communist Party of the Soviet Union* (New York: Random House, 1960), p. 508.

Benes, Masaryk's heir, turned over Czechoslovakia's eastern province, Ruthenia, with its largely Ukrainian population, to the USSR with the clear inference that the rest of the nation was outside Soviet domination. In May 1946, the Czechs held free elections in which the Communists received 2.7 million out of 7.1 million votes, and the Party formed a coalition government with the Social Democrats.

Unfortunately, the Czech Social Democrats were led by a "mole," Zdenek Fierlinger, who had been secretly recruited to the Communist movement during his tenure as Czech Ambassador to Moscow.[131] While this was to prove crucial later, in 1947 Jan Masaryk, Foreign Minister and son of Thomas, was apparently unaware that Czechoslovakia had lost its sovereignty. In July he had the effrontery to accept an invitation for Czechoslovakia to attend the Marshall Plan Conference in Paris at which Western European nations, led by Britain's Foreign Secretary Ernest Bevin, organized their response to the American offer of aid for reconstruction. Moscow immediately fired a rocket at Prague, and Communist Prime Minister Klement Gottwald kept Masaryk from participating. The Poles, who had initially shown interest, were similarly restrained.

In February 1948, Stalin decided to end the masked ball, and Klement Gottwald led a Communist coup with the full cooperation of "Social Democratic" Minister of the Interior Fierlinger.[132] In March, Jan Masaryk, according to reliable sources, committed suicide on being pushed from his office window. President Benes, with his characteristic "Good Soldier Schweik" approach to life, then gave his blessing to the Stalinist seizure of power. When queried by an American acquaintance on his passivity, Benes observed soulfully, "We must not forget that Prague, beautiful Prague, was the only major European city not destroyed by World War II bombing."[133]

There is no point in exploring the period between Stalin's consolidation of his sphere of power (and the notorious subsequent purges in Eastern Europe) in 1948 and his death in 1953, except to note there were a number of fierce diplomatic encounters as the United States worked toward the rebuilding and eventual rearming of an integrated Western Europe. Most of these encounters focused on the place of Germany—

---

[131]See Denis W. Healey, editor, *The Curtain Falls: The Story of the Socialists in Eastern Europe* (London: Lincolns-Prager, 1951), pp. 89-90. This section of the book was written by Vaclav Majer, a Socialist Minister in the Czech Government from 1945 to 1948, who quotes Fierlinger's memoirs and drew on his own experience.

[132]See Borkenau, *op. cit.*, p. 534.

[133]Quoted by Raymond Aron in *The Committed Observer* (Chicago, Ill.: Regnery-Gateway, 1983), p. 57. See also Vojtech Mastny, *The Czechs under Nazi Rule* (New York: Columbia University Press, 1971), p. 19, and Edward Taborsky, *President Edvard Beneš Between East and West* (Stanford, Calif.: Hoover Institution Press, 1981).

or, of the Germanies. The high point was the Soviet blockade of Berlin from July 1948 to May 1949. This was overcome by the American airlift, which could easily have been blocked by a determined Soviet policy. But the ever-cautious Stalin—having struck at a target of opportunity with a built-in fail-safe mechanism—quietly backed away, and was applauded by "progressives" for his restraint!

Before turning to the impact of these Soviet policies on the worldwide Communist movement, we should take a quick look at the Korean War of June 1950. American right-wing oratory to the contrary notwithstanding, Stalin took a dim view of Chinese communism. As a spokesman for Soviet national interests, he had a vested interest in a weak China and in that respect found the Nationalist Government of Chiang Kai-shek ideal. Thus, while he put up a major, successful battle for admitting his client Polish Provisional Government to the United Nations in 1945, he never made the slightest effort to promote the interests of Mao Tse-tung's Chinese counterpart in Yenan. Nor did he object to Chiang's regime filling the permanent Security Council seat assigned to China.

Soviet behavior in Manchuria after their last-minute entrance into the war against Japan, on August 9, 1945, further buttresses the proposition that Stalin considered Mao's movement marginal. Manchuria, a Chinese province seized by Japan and developed into the Japanese Ruhr, was stripped by the Soviets of all industrial equipment and infrastructural material down to railroad tracks and ties.

If they had had any vested interest in a Chinese Communist victory in the immediate future, this was—to say the least—most uncomradely behavior. A devastated Manchuria was returned to the theoretical sovereignty of the Republic of China. No conciliatory effort was made to return the Mongolian People's Republic, stolen from China in 1919, or Tannu Tuva, grabbed in 1944, to Stalin's Chinese allies—either to Chiang's Nationalists or to Mao's Communists. In short, the evidence indicates that Mao's consolidation of power on Mainland China between 1945-50 was accomplished with little Soviet aid and with considerable surprise to Moscow.[134]

This leads us to the perplexing question: Did Stalin "order" Kim Il-sung's North Korea to invade the South? In his memoirs, Nikita Khrushchev says that Kim raised the matter with Stalin who was noncommittal,

---

[134]A point most recently made by Deng Xiaoping in an interview with the Italian journalist Oriana Fallaci. Queried about Stalin's standing in the Chinese People's Republic, Deng replied, "We think that Stalin's merits and contributions to the revolution exceed his mistakes. . . . When, after the Second World War, there was a rupture between the Chinese Communist Party and the Kuomintang and we engaged in the Liberation war, Stalin was against us." *Manchester Guardian*, September 28, 1980, p. 17.

essentially saying, "Try it if you want, but don't count on me."[135] Despite the questionable provenance of Khrushchev's memoirs, the story has a certain plausibility: Korea was another target of opportunity (like Berlin) where Stalin had a fail-safe scenario.

First, would the Americans respond? In the summer of 1949, the Joint Chiefs of Staff had prepared a map of American vital interests in the Pacific and, with the full agreement of our Japanese Viceroy, Douglas MacArthur, excluded the Korean peninsula from its scope. This map was used by Secretary of State Dean Acheson in his famous National Press Club speech of January 1950, and led to subsequent charges that Acheson had invited Kim's invasion.[136]

Second, in February 1950, Stalin was suddenly recognizing the genius of Mao, who came to Moscow on the 14th to sign a 30-year Treaty of Friendship, Alliance, and Mutual Assistance with the USSR and to receive extensive promises of economic and military aid, including the development of nuclear arms. Thus, by June of 1950, when Kim's army struck the Republic of Korea, Stalin had calculated that his new Chinese friends would be available to handle any untoward events in the Korean War. This is not speculation: since the Sino-Soviet break, Chinese spokesmen have bitterly attacked the way Stalin tricked them into pulling his Korean chestnuts out of the fire.[137]

In the event, at an enormous cost in casualties (reliable estimates suggest over one million were killed), the Chinese People's Republic rescued North Korea while the Soviet Union watched benignly and provided a few MiG-17s to engage U.S. F-86s in "MiG Alley," antique T-34 tanks, and other miscellaneous ordnance. When all was said and done and the hostilities ceased, it was the Chinese, not the Soviets, who had carried the burden. Moscow mounted a propaganda offensive through the World Peace Council and its subsidiaries, but nobody died in this agit-prop exercise.

To return to the main line of analysis and complete the overview, from the time Nazi Germany's defeat was certain in early 1945, which signaled the demise of "Browderism" or "class collaborationism" in all its manifestations, to his death in 1953, Stalin was dedicated to the Cold War with

---

[135]Nikita Khrushchev, *Khrushchev Remembers* (Boston: Little Brown, 1970), pp. 367-373.

[136]David Rees, *Korea: The Limited War* (New York: St. Martin's, 1964), pp. 13-20.

[137]A number of official American visitors to the PRC since our recognition of Beijing have reported bitter diatribes by leaders of the People's Liberation Army against Stalin's treachery. James Schlesinger and Richard Perle got an earful, which they related to me; and several PLA visitors to the Fletcher School, under "light cover" as representatives of PRC foreign policy and defense think tanks, have given me blow-by-blow descriptions. One senior officer said he took a regiment into Korea and emerged with a company!

49

the West (with Korea as a, perhaps unforeseen, "hot" war). From the time the West awoke, roughly coincidental with the Truman Doctrine of March 1947 and the Marshall Plan in June, the world Stalinist movement was orchestrated to block "imperialism."

In the United States this was manifested in the formation in January 1947 of the Progressive Citizens of America, with former Vice President and Secretary of Commerce Henry A. Wallace as its figurehead. In 1948, Wallace ran for President on the Progressive Party ticket with no notable impact: he received 2.38 percent of the vote and tipped New York, Michigan, and Maryland into Thomas E. Dewey's column, but Truman was reelected. Stalinist-dominated trade unions in the Congress of Industrial Organizations (CIO) urged both political and industrial action (notably among the maritime and longshoremen's unions) to block Marshall Plan aid, but were stone-walled by CIO and federal action.[138]

In Western Europe, notably France, where the major trade union center, the *Confédération Générale de Travail* (CGT), was a wholly owned subsidiary of the PCF, the play was considerably rougher.[139] However, in a period when Social Democrats still remembered vividly the murder and betrayal of their comrades by the Stalinists, a series of French Socialist Ministers of the Interior—notably, Jules Moch—suppressed illegal strike action. And, encouraged by the American Federation of Labor's Free Trade Union committee, the Socialist workers split away from the CGT in 1947 to found a rival center, the *Force Ouvrière*. A parallel split took place in Italy in both the fellow-traveling Socialist Party and the Communist trade union center, the General Confederation of Italian Workers (CGIL).

In Britain the Labour Party, in power from 1945 to 1951, had some internal problems with its left-wingers. It was a bit embarrassing to have Professor Harold Laski, the former Chairman of the Labour Party's National Executive Committee, writing in a French Communist weekly that Truman was the greatest menace to the peace since Hitler, and at least twenty Members of Parliament had problems distinguishing left from east.[140] In 1948-49, four devout fellow-travelers (including one Titoite!) were expelled from the Parliamentary Labour Party and lost

---

[138]See Max Kampleman, *The Communist Party vs. the C.I.O.* (New York: Arno and the New York Times, 1971).

[139]See Mario Einaudi, *Communism in Western Europe* (Ithaca, N.Y.: Cornell University Press, 1951); John Windmuller, *American Labor and the International Labor Movement, 1940-1953* (Ithaca, N.Y.: Cornell University Press, 1954); Roy Godson, *American Labor and European Policies* (New York: Crane, Russak, 1976).

[140]"Laski Répond à Truman: La Plus grande Menace pour la Paix depuis Hitler," *Action* (Paris), March 28, 1947, No. 130, p. 2.

their seats in 1950, as did the independent crypto-Communist Member, D. N. Pritt.[141]

Prime Minister Clement Attlee and Foreign Secretary Ernest Bevin, the latter a scarred veteran of fighting against Communist efforts to disrupt both the Trades Union Congress (TUC) and his own Transport Workers' Union, were in no mood to play games with Stalinists. When the Labour Party proscribed a list of over twenty-five Communist front groups, it was accused of "witch-hunting." Bevin's blunt reply was "there never were witches, but Commie bastards have been around for thirty years."[142] Some British unions, notably the Miners led by Communist Arthur Horner, supported French political strikes, but in October 1948 the General Council of the TUC voted that "Statements made by the Communist Party in Britain prove beyond question that sabotage of the European Recovery Plan [Marshall Plan] is its present aim."[143]

The TUC sent out a pamphlet, *Defend Democracy*, to all unions indicating that Party members and fellow-travelers were subversives and that "the party centre, which directs the whole of these subversive activities, exists outside the trade union movement."[144] The battle continued in some unions with strong Communist cells—for example, there was cooperation between Communist-dominated Canadian seamen and *apparatchiks* in the British Transport Workers to block the unloading of Marshall Plan goods, but the unofficial strike disintegrated when the British longshoremen realized that they were being duped. However, at the top level, the Annual Conference of the TUC in September 1949, the strong policy of the General Council was endorsed nine to one. In the unions the Communists were either barred from leadership or went to ground; by 1950 all was quiet on the disruptive front.

The narrative could continue with a travelogue of Communist efforts all the way from Australia—where they were strong in transport—to Zanzibar—where they were apparently uninterested in cloves—but everywhere the script was the same. The various parties, with expulsions here and there (in Norway, for example), shifted from the cooperative line of June 1941 to Stalin's new "general line" of April 1945 when the Duclos assault on "Browderism" appeared, and became "anti-imperialist," anti-American instruments.

---

[141]See David Caute, *The Fellow-Travellers* (New York: Macmillan, 1973), p. 224.

[142]Related to me about 1954 by Denis W. Healey, M.P., who in the immediate postwar years was the Labour Party's International Representative, working closely with Bevin. Healey was a spectacular mimic; I only wish I could reproduce accurately his imitation of Bevin's Bristol workingclass cadences.

[143]See Henry Pelling, *The British Communist Party* (London: Adam and Charles Black, 1958), p. 154.

[144]*Ibid.*, p. 158.

To summarize, by the time of Stalin's death in 1953, Marxist-Leninist techniques of organization were as rigidly stylized as classical Russian ballet. When the ballet director issued the script, the cadres went into action, "transmission belts" whined, and "innocents' clubs" popped up like mushrooms devoted to "Saving the Rosenbergs," or "Hands off Cuba," or "Recognize the NLF," (or PLO, or Sandinistas, or East Timor Liberation Movement, in recent years.)

Often these movements utilized a legitimate grievance to rally support—which is why it is defamatory to call all their supporters Communists. But the human capacity to be duped must never be underestimated, particularly when practiced and cynical cadres employ the vocabulary of high morality. Cuban dictator Batista, like his Nicaraguan counterpart Somoza, was a stench in the nostrils of humanity, but in realistic terms, both were amateur totalitarians when compared with their Soviet-sponsored successors.

3.
Epilogue

THERE HAVE been innumerable books published on the various activities of the Communist movement, and they present a historiographical pattern of great interest. Disregarding agit-prop tracts, serious analyses written before roughly 1960 echoed or documented the work of the great Franz Borkenau on the action of the Comintern.[145] The death of Stalin, and Khrushchev's subsequent "revelations" of the Georgian dictator's barbarism at the Soviet Twentieth Party Congress in 1956, led to a virtual Pentacostal orgy in which old, barnacled *apparatchiks* and veteran fellow-travelers filled the pages of books and journals with their wails of disillusionment.[146] Their self-flagellation was additionally humiliating, since those of us who were not startled by Khrushchev's epiphany but thought that he had grossly understated the case were sardonically cheering from the grandstands.

In short, we considered the Communists to be ideological whores, part of a highly articulated, worldwide criminal syndicate with its Godfather resident in the Kremlin. Its major objective was not to win the hearts and minds of mankind with the altruistic apothegms of Marx and Lenin, but to achieve power at whatever levels in institutions that presented themselves as targets of opportunity. The motivation for their activities was not to improve the caloric intake of the "wretched of the earth"—indeed, as Cuba indicates, they can take a flourishing economy on the verge of "take-off" and in record time convert it into an outdoor slum wholly dependent on Moscow's handouts—but to buttress in one fashion or another the international position of the Soviet Union.

For the benefit of the younger generation, this would be the time to formulate some crucial distinctions among anti-Communists. The men and women I am talking about (who have been my lifetime friends and associates) must not be lumped with the anti-Communist primitives who

---

[145]See his *The Communist International* (London: Faber and Faber Limited, 1938), and *European Communism* (London: Faber, 1953).

[146]My favorite piece in this genre is the *mea culpa* of I.F. Stone in *I.F. Stone's Weekly*, May 28, 1956. This first line conveys the mood: "The way home from Moscow has been agony for me." By the time he concludes, there is not a dry eye in the house. (Unless some cruel old anti-Stalinists have slipped in to point out that, for example, the *Free Trade Union News*, monthly of the AFL's Free Trade Union Committee, published in 1947 what Solzhenitsyn later described as a remarkably accurate map of Stalin's "Gulag Archipelago.") Ironically, a few days later Joseph Clark, then foreign editor of the *Daily Worker* but later himself to jump ship, took Stone severely to task for writing "an essay on Lenin and Leninism which is embarrassing in its ignorance." June 1, 1956, pp. 5, 8.

specialized in scarifying "Godless, atheistical, anti-capitalist Bolsheviks." These critics made the mistake of taking Marxism-Leninism at face value as a philosophy, rather than as an operational code for taking power.

For example, the Eastern Orthodox Patriarch of Moscow in 1983 rallied his Metropolitans and Archpriests for a public display of religious wrath against NATO's deployment of Pershing IIs and cruise missiles. The photograph dramatically highlighted the immense pectoral silver crosses against the backdrop of black vestments. Whether or not, as is rumored, the Patriarch is a KGB Major General hardly alters the fact that in outward and visible terms Yuri Andropov did not appear to be a member of the League of the Militant Godless.

As far as capitalism is concerned, Moscow's mafia can take it or leave it alone depending on the calculus of interest. In Angola (Cabinda) at the moment, Cuban sepoys of the Marxist-Leninist MPLA government are defending Gulf Oil's extensive operations against black nationalist guerrillas. (It is seldom realized that the MPLA elite is a creation of what was known as Portugal's first 500-year plan: *assimilados* who had been educated in Lisbon and comprised the urban mulatto leadership. The overwhelming black majority refers to them contemptuously as "brown Portuguese.")

In a different context, leading American capitalists have found a warm welcome in Moscow—the Chase Manhattan Bank is located on Karl Marx Prospekt—and the KGB has shown a far greater interest in stealing capitalist creations than in shooting up Silicon Valley. Certainly the Soviet leadership is as opposed to the free market as it is to freedom in any other sphere, but the notion that Marxism-Leninism is an economic crusade is sheer nonsense. The cult of austerity among the *nomenklatura* (top bureaucracy) ended with Lenin and Trotsky: Svetlana Stalin's description of her father's sybaritic tastes will match anything "degenerate capitalism" has to offer.[147]

In this connection, it is interesting to note that Grigory V. Romanov, one of the leading contenders in the post-Andropov leadership derby, was gently "gigged" by former *Vozd* Leonid Brezhnev for an uproarious event at his daughter's wedding. Romanov, then Leningrad Party chief, had borrowed Catherine the Great's china service from the Hermitage Museum for the occasion, and the wedding party, whether animated by alcohol or anti-Czarist passion, topped off the celebration by shattering it. Andropov, perhaps operating on the maxim that *apparatchiks* have to have a little fun, promoted him to the Central Committee in June 1983.

---

[147]Svetlana Allileva, *Twenty Letters to a Friend*, translated by Priscilla Johnson McMillan (New York: Harper, 1967).

Veteran, professional analysts of the Communist movement have always kept their focus on organizational activities rather than on slogans. The early Stalinist interest in Hollywood, for example, was not designed to insert agit-prop into the movies (*Mission to Moscow* was the only World War II film that overtly sustained the Party line; others such as *North Star* merely reflected the over-reaction of the American people to the unquestionable bravery of the Russian people under Nazi assault.) No, as noted earlier, Willi's *apparat* headed for Hollywood because that was where the money was: it was a generous "milk cow."

No one knows how many millions were extracted from rich, simple souls who gave to the Hollywood Anti-Nazi Committee, or the Hollywood branch of the American League for Peace and Democracy, or the Friends of the Abraham Lincoln Brigade, or any of the other fronts. Only the Communist hierarchy knows how it was spent. *Apparatchiks* emeriti, once highly placed, have informed me that no more than 10 to 15 percent of the money raised went into anti-Nazi activities. The remainder went to sustain the cadres, the organizers of anti-Nazi fundraisers. Moreover, funds were fungible: money raised in Hollywood for the League for Peace and Democracy could be spent by the Party "center" to support the infrastructure of the Committee for a Democratic Far Eastern Policy. Willi's "trust" was not annually audited.

Perhaps a personal experience will help emphasize the total cynicism of the Stalinist *modus operandi*. In 1940, when I was in college and also immersed in the work of the Young People's Socialist League, we were militantly opposed to American involvement in World War II. One of our problems was that the Stalinists were, as devotees of the Stalin-Hitler Pact, also anti-war and kept trying to infiltrate our organizations, for example, the Youth Committee Against War.

They were constantly attempting to set up a united anti-war front— the present Bella Abzug, then a student at Hunter College, was among their most active leaders—and we had to be ready at any function or rally for a takeover effort. This meant I could not go home early, but I still had to do my college homework as well as put in twenty hours each week to the National Youth Administration to pay for my textbooks. One night, in a rage, I turned to an old-time Socialist sage and asked, "How can these troublemakers hang around all night? Don't they have to make money to stay in school?"

He smiled wryly and said, "John, you don't understand; they are all insurance men." I looked baffled, so he filled me in: "They are all carried on the payroll of the IWO [International Workers' Order] or one of its satellites. They may not collect much insurance, but they have their nights free." The IWO was a Communist split from the Jewish Socialist Workmen's Circle, which in the era before the welfare state, provided rudimentary insurance and burial costs. A member would pay, perhaps, five cents a week for a stamp to put in a membership book. But the IWO, unlike the Workmen's Circle, branched out to set up facilities for a wide range of ethnic groups, e.g., the Finnish People's Fraternal Order, the Jewish People's Fraternal Order, etc. It was a masterly umbrella *apparat*, and had patronage: there were always jobs for insurance collectors, lawyers, accountants, and administrators. Needless to say, the IWO was not, in political terms, an affirmative action employer.

Thus, my generation of liberal or democratic socialist anticommunists were immunized against the notion that Stalinists were merely (as current obituaries of dedicated *apparatchiks* put it) "radical activists." We knew that John Dos Passos' *Adventures of a Young Man*,[148] while admittedly not an artistic masterpiece, accurately portrayed the savage treatment the Soviet hit-men in the International Brigades dealt out to dissidents against Moscow. We read George Orwell's *Homage to Catalonia*,[149] in which the treatment accorded by the Spanish Stalinists to militantly anti-Franco Catalans was pungently chronicled. We knew relatives of young idealists who had gone to Spain to fight for the Republic and were murdered in the OGPU's private prison at Alcala de Henares outside Madrid for allegedly being "Trotskyite-Franco-Nazi agents and provocateurs."[150]

Finally, when persons such as Joseph McCarthy came along in the late 1940s and early 1950s, we considered them albatrosses around our necks: their frenetic activities simply gave anticommunism a bad name. In entrepreneurial circles "blacklisting" became a growth industry, a variety of legalized blackmail. Some "useful idiot" who had signed petitions or public advertisements urging, say, "A Second Front Now!," or who had contributed to the Hollywood Anti-Nazi Committee, or supported the American Writers' Congress, the American Student Union, Henry Wallace, or the League Against War and Fascism, without remotely understanding their ancestry, would be told his job was in jeopardy, that he was a "Comsymp."

There were some honest fanatics in the blacklisting business, but it is fair to say that absolution was generally provided by the Inquisitors after

---

[148](Boston: Houghton Mifflin, 1938).

[149](London: Secker and Warburg, 1938). *Homage* itself became a bit of a legend: the original printing was small and it shortly vanished from the public scene. As Harcourt, Brace did not bring out an American edition until 1952, back in the late 1930s and 1940s copies of the English edition were passed from hand to hand in the United States almost like *samizdat* works in the Soviet Union. Before lending a copy, one did a full field check on the character of the borrower. Readers under forty have no idea what life was like in the pre-Xerox era.

[150]See my "Remembering the Levitas Salon," *op. cit.*

a ritual of penance that could become rather expensive. In the long run, the activities of the blacklisters were even more insidious: because they painted with such a broad brush, and the charges were often patently trivial, they discredited those who were concerned with spotting and countering the activities of the authentic cadres. The blacklist, to mix metaphors, provided a smokescreen: like Nixon's 1952 accusation that "Adlai Stevenson the appeaser . . . got a Ph.D. from Dean Acheson's College of Cowardly Communist Containment," wild charges of pro-Stalinism led to the depreciation of the currency of analytical discourse. Later, as we shall see, it provided a new generation with a Pavlovian tic: anyone who was accused by Nixon—or anybody else—must have been innocent, a victim of "red-baiting" and a "witch-hunt."[151]

While this has wandered a bit, and is frankly an *apologia pro vita mea*, I think it essential to understand that the major contribution the Stalinists made to American politics was (like the Leninist world model) organizational, not substantive. In the 1950s and 1960s friends would call me up as a consultant (unpaid) on whether or not to support some cause which appealed to their sense of social justice. My first question was always, "Who is the executive director?," and my second, "Who is the secretary-treasurer?" (Once in the 1950s I spotted a character who was executive director of eleven Communist Party fronts, all operating from the same office.)

Beginning in the 1960s, as the generational factor began inexorably to operate, such questions as these seemed to some to display an uncaring, mechanical approach to life. If I responded to a question about a petition attacking South African *apartheid*, Pakistani martial law, discrimination against the Tamils in Sri Lanka, or the building of a nuclear reactor in the Harvard Yard by asking who were the executive director and secretary-treasurer, the characteristic response would be, "But what about the issues?" If I said, truthfully, that I was opposed to the behavior in at least three instances, the reply would be, "Then, what difference does it make who sponsored it?"

Perhaps each generation has to learn the fundamentals by experience. After all, I was allegedly an intelligent young man, but it took Pearl Harbor to pluck me out of my generational narcissus bed, and until about 1943 I thought the horror stories of Hitler's "Final Solution" of the

---

[151]Watergate and the disgrace of Nixon stimulated a growth industry: the attempted rehabilitation of anyone ever accused of being a Stalinist operative. Alger Hiss and the Rosenbergs were the most notable instances. Accompanying these specific efforts at retroactive beatification was a flood of literature on the extent of terrorism and repression in the "McCarthy era." For my contemporary views on the anticommunist "reign of terror," see my series in the *New Republic*, "We've Never Had More Freedom," January 23, January 30, and February 6, 1956. For a later recap, see my review of David Caute's *The Great Fear*, in *Political Science Quarterly*, Summer 1979, pp. 361-362.

"problem" of European Jewry were British propaganda, a rerun of the British propaganda spectacular of World War I, "The Rape of Belgium."

Be that as it may, the fact is that today well over half the population of the United States was born after World War II and grew up in a world in which the Soviet Union and the United States are largely seen as status quo powers. Mass education at the college level has produced an educated elite that is essentially *déraciné*, if not blatantly anti-American. It constitutes a small percentage of the grateful total, but has seized the role of the generational "vanguard." You could fill a substantial hall at a meeting of American historians, for example, with scribes who are convinced that the Cold War was invented by "warmongers" (like me) as an excuse for creating "the American Century." On the basic level, they are not pro-Soviet, but they enjoy their narcissus bed and are afraid that vigorous American leadership in opposition to Marxism-Leninism will disturb it.

The organizational savvy that the New Left has picked up from the Old has been given an exponential potential by television. If five militants get around a table, they can work out a protest agenda to appeal to a disparate set of constituencies. A classic from the 1930s involved an increase in fees at Brooklyn College. The National Student League, the American branch of the international Communist youth organization (Willi Münzenberg's first creation), decided to use the fee raise as the basis for a monster student rally. The signs read: "Fight Imperialist War/NSL Protests Expulsion of its Delegates to Kentucky/NSL Fights Discrimination Against Negro Students/Free Tom Mooney/Down With Fees."[152]

The rally was apparently a flop, but next time you see the displays at some protest rally, look for the mélange. Typically on Boston Common there will be a set ranging from the nuclear freeze to "End Police Brutality in Dorchester." Moreover, the rally and television cameras (properly employed) were born for each other. On a TV close-up, you hear the roars of anguish from the oppressed masses; they are practically climbing out of the set into your living room. A wide pan, however, may well demonstrate that sixty synchronized screamers were clustered around the camera.

Television has become a potent weapon in the organizational battle, and it is less than a conspiracy but more than an accident that the television industry has been a magnetic field for the talented, *déraciné* "new class" of intellectuals, a comfortable and lucrative base for the "vanguard."

Perhaps the best example of employing television in the service of "new class" values was the movie *The Day After*, shown by the American Broad-

---

[152]Cited in Thomas E. Coulton, *A City College in Action* (New York: Harpers, 1955), p. 105.

casting Company on November 20, 1983. ABC vigorously denied that its portrayal of the radioactivation of Kansas City and Lawrence, Kansas, was in any way "political," although it was aired at the precise time that NATO and the Soviet Union were eyeball-to-eyeball over the deployment of Pershing IIs and cruise missiles in Europe—in response to the massive Soviet deployment of SS-20 missiles.

Brandon Stoddard, head of ABC's Motion Picture Division, discussed this charge on CBS' "Sixty Minutes" on November 13, and was baffled by it: "I'll say again and again that it's not [political]. It was never intended to be, and it isn't. It is a movie that says nuclear war is horrible. That's what it says."

However, the film's director, Nicholas Meyer, had earlier undermined this altar boy posture: at a press conference in New York he admitted he was involved in the antinuclear movement and went so far as to suggest that *The Day After* might turn out to be the *Uncle Tom's Cabin* of the nuclear abolitionists. In a *TV Guide* article, he signaled the difference between the men and the boys in the agit-prop business.[153]

Willi Münzenberg surely knew the Nazis did not burn down the *Reichstag*, but he would never have admitted it. Meyer in *TV Guide* noted ingenuously, "My own antinuclear bias must be set aside. If the film is perceived as propaganda it will be useless." He would not have lasted three months in Willi's "trust": such egotistical introspection, narcissism, was "objectively counter-revolutionary." But the fact that the antinuclear orchestration is not a Münzenberg set-piece does not lessen its impact. Indeed, it may enhance it.

Given the widespread process of imitation, the organizational techniques devised by the Marxist-Leninists now appear at every point on the political spectrum. Indeed, one of life's ironies is that political action committees (PACs) which used to be virtually a liberal monopoly (when I was National Chairman of Americans for Democratic Action we used to set up a dozen a year) have now been adopted, and brilliantly employed, by American conservatives. Similarly, I suspect the "right to life" and "right to choice" organizations are probably operational clones.

Many years ago, while exploring medieval political theory, I propounded "Roche's Law of Hierarchical Stability" which hypothesized that in any unstable situation, the first entity to get its act together would serve as the model for its competitors. Thus, the administrative reforms instituted in the eleventh century Catholic Church by Pope Gregory VII, which broke the ecclesiological pattern of feudal fragmentation of power,

---

[153]Quoted in Reed Irvine, editor, *AIM Report*, Vol. XII, No. 23, December 1983. For an appraisal of the impact and motivation of the media elite that converges with mine in emphasizing its lack of deep ideological roots, see Austin Ranney, *Channels of Power* (New York: Basic Books, 1983).

were promptly imitated by ambitious secular rulers, and later an absolutist church supplied the paradigm for mundane absolutism.

(Interestingly enough, the restrictions placed upon multinational corporations in the contemporary developing world parallel efforts in the Middle Ages to curb the multinational church: the fight between Popes and Kings over the right to appoint bishops—the "Investiture Controversy"—was a prefiguring of demands by, say, India to appoint the directors of the Indian subsidiary of IBM.)

The point of this foray into the past is to emphasize that, just as plagiarism is the most sincere form of flattery, imitation is a tribute to the cleverness of those who designed the vanguard, cadre party. This becomes relevant to the analysis of such phenomena as the demand for a nuclear freeze. Of course, as John Barron has documented,[154] the international Communist movement kicked it off through the World Peace Council, and there is evidence that, particularly in the Federal Republic of Germany, a good deal of money has appeared from unidentified sources to cultivate the "spontaneous" drive against NATO's missile deployment. An East German "professor," Arwid Spreu, was expelled from Holland and later Belgium when authorities found he had 200,000 comradely dollars in his attaché case targeted for the "peace" movements in those nations.

But this funding, as well as the organizational expertise of Communist and new left cadres, would be useless if it did not mesh with spontaneous, disorganized narcissism. A veteran Comintern *apparatchik* who watched the huge undisciplined demonstrations, whether in West Germany or Central Park, would have a fit and promptly write a denunciation of the "petty bourgeois romanticism" of the organizers. Stalin shot anyone who used the word "spontaneous." (This obviously does not apply to the thugs who engage in deliberate police provocations to start a riot, but they have been largely unsuccessful as the police become better trained and more sophisticated.)

An argument could be made that since the 1960s political rallies have served libidinous objectives far better than political ones: they are perfect cheap dates. As a clinical witness to several mass rallies, beginning with the one at the Pentagon in October 1967, I have gained the distinct impression that, however dour and dedicated the cadres, the masses consisted of boys and girls, or men and women, who wanted to make love, not agit-prop. Judging from the amount of contraceptive detritus cleaned up by the Park Service after the Pentagon affair, a significant number of dissenting idealists joyfully mixed business with pleasure. It

---

[154]*The KGB Today: The Hidden Hand* (New York: Reader's Digest Press, 1983), pp. 249-293.

was hardly accidental that great religious revivals in early American history invariably generated big jumps in the illegitimate birthrate.

What a U.S. President or a German Chancellor should realize is that, while Boris Ponomarev's merry men of the "ghost Comintern" (the International Department of the Soviet Central Committee) are working day and night to destabilize the NATO alliance, they no longer have the allegiance of influential *organized* mass organizations. In 1939, for example, Stalinist cadres controlled at least a dozen trade unions in the United States:[155] the General Counsel of the Congress of Industrial Organizations, Lee Pressman; the CIO National Director of Organization, John Brophy; and the Editor of the CIO *News*, Len DeCaux—all were dutiful *apparatchiks*.[156] Today, with the possible exception of the West Coast Longshoremen and Meat Cutters, Moscow has not a friend in the American "House of Labor." Similarly, the German unions are anticommunist, and union centers elsewhere are surviving by emphasizing bread and butter issues.

It is, therefore, perfectly accurate to say that the Communists are behind the demand for a nuclear freeze, but it is something quite different to say that supporters of the freeze movement are procommunist. Some are, but again remember (and every generation tends to think the country is populated by his or her cohort) the demographics: most Americans have grown up in a world where Hitler, Stalin, and World War II are thought of as medieval history. A simple litmus test: gather twenty bright college graduates and ask them, "How did the United States get into World War II?" They probably learned from the TV series, "The Winds of War," that the Japanese attacked Pearl Harbor, but when you point out that December 7 got us into war only with Japan, a strange stillness sets in. Try it: see how many of our best and brightest know Hitler declared war on us on December 11, 1941.

What the Communists can do is play on an ancient American theme:

---

[155]See Kampelman, *op. cit.*

[156]Howe and Cose, *op. cit.*, p. 374. Pressman was the Communist Party's "control" at the sessions of the Progressive Party's Platform Committee in 1948, and extremely efficient at guiding that collection of ex-New Dealers, like Henry Wallace motivated by their hatred for the "usurper" Truman more than by great pro-Moscow zeal, to a set of anti-anticommunist resolutions. But even Homer nods: one day when Pressman was out to lunch, a petitioner came before the Committee with an impassioned plea for Macedonian self-determination. How could any true Progressive reject Macedonian self-determination? It was unanimously put in the Wallace Platform. When Pressman returned, he discovered that Chairman Rex Tugwell had permitted a "Trotskyite-Titoist-Bukharinite" heresy to slip by—at that time the Cominform line was that there were no Macedonians, only "Western Bulgarians"—and somehow the printed version of the Committee's recommendations that went to the whole Convention dropped this plank. There was a rumor I will neither confirm nor deny that the "Macedonian" was dispatched upon his mission by the recently formed Americans for Democratic Action: my hazy personal recollection is that he was actually a Hungarian Socialist refugee who worked in a Philadelphia restaurant.

isolationism, which is the political version of self-centeredness. The young need little urging because in fact their response to contemporary world issues is as American as apple pie. My generation—I call it the Class of 1941—which was born during or shortly after World War I and grew up in the Great Depression was traumatized into internationalism by the events of December 1941.

We became the first internationalist generation in the nation's history, as in the postwar period we rebuilt Europe and Japan, entered entangling alliances, e.g., NATO, and undertook—in the words our generation's President, John F. Kennedy, was to use in Dallas the night he was murdered—to be the "watchmen on the walls of world freedom." In this role we became involved in the most unselfish war in our history: Vietnam. It was a war fought for an abstraction, the containment of totalitarianism, in a place most Americans had never heard of, and as the bodies came home, the old collective instinct revived: "What are we doing over *there*?"

The myth subsequently arose that left-wing demonstrations convinced the American people to repudiate the Vietnam War (presumably by electing Richard Nixon President!), but as all serious polls indicated, the rationale was isolationist. As an old Boston Irish pol summarized it, "My people want to end the war, and shoot the draft-dodgers." In a phrase, patriotic isolationism—he could have been my father talking politics in the 1930s.

To summarize, the influence of Marxist-Leninist organizational theory has been so diffused that what we see in the United States is not a left-wing, anti-American monolith, but dozens of groups organized on a nuclear model but with ad hoc, undisciplined relations with each other and no GHQ. Paradoxically, while they mouth radical slogans, their constituents are *psychologically* conservative: young people who do not want to die for anyone's freedom, and their isolationist elders.

With this in mind, it is wise to be extremely skeptical of conspiracy theories. But on a different axis, the "new class" learned a very important lesson from the Marxist-Leninists, namely, if you want to be effective, find the fuse box and tie up the important circuits. In my time, as noted earlier, the key posts in any organization were the executive director and the secretary-treasurer. Now, with the immense increase in federal and state bureaucracies, to say nothing of private religious and charitable groups, the key slots for influencing policy are at the staff level. Unseemly as it may sound, I have seen members of the United States Senate rushing to a floor vote look to a staffer for the thumb: up = yes; down = no.

What the "new class"—an unnervingly large percentage of them lawyers—has done is to colonize bureaucracies. I will for reasons of space skip over the private sector (though detective work might lead to some interesting information on who provides newspaper editors with "the spike" or Catholic bishops or foundation directors with "the thumb") and confine my speculation to the federal government. It should be made clear at the outset that my observations are clinical, not polemical: we are not talking about violations of the Criminal Code. (John Barron has dealt masterfully with the espionage and other activities of the KGB, which are outside the purview of this study.)

What these frequently very talented young people share is an essentially esthetic anti-Americanism. I recall similar reactions in the 1950s founded on the premise that only a nation of clods could elect Eisenhower over Stevenson; indeed, I noted at the time that Stevenson's great appeal to the intellectuals was not his politics (he was actually quite conservative) but his almost Athenian persona.[157]

Once we realize that Greeks hated Romans, we have, in a Jungian sense, spotted the gravamen of the new class' hostility to the political process, American style. (Plato's guardians and Lenin's vanguard would, however, have few problems understanding each other.) The nation, they feel, is run by a collection of self-interested dimwits who seem to believe that the populace has a better grasp of the "public interest" than its natural leaders, the enlightened, disinterested experts.

This view was confirmed by the magistral authority of Arthur Ochs ("Punch") Sulzberger, President and Chairman of the *New York Times* in a June 1983 interview. At issue was the right of the press to leak government secrets; the interviewer, Reed Irving of Accuracy In Media, took issue with Sulzberger's view that the media had the final say on whether leaking such material was in the national interest. Sulzberger's reply: "Yes, after 102 years of publishing we think that we do basically a better job at it [defining the national interest] than those elected officials who go out every four years."[158] The inference is that, sadly, elections are still held.

He, like other media moguls, must have been stunned by the public's reaction to the exclusion of reporters from the initial stages of the liberation of Grenada, which showed—to put it in worst-case terms—that the populace distrusted journalists even more than they did the government.

The obvious solution to this wretched state of affairs is for the virtuous experts to move in on the "political class"—to use Gaetano Mosca's term—and gently provide policy guidance. After all, the members of the political

---

[157]See my "Can Kennedy Set Them Afire?," *New Republic*, September 26, 1960.

[158]Reed Irvine, *AIM Report*, Vol. XII, No. 15, August 1983. A superb analysis of the pretensions of the "new class" is Roger Sandall, "Guardianship," *Quadrant*, April 1983, pp. 79-84.

class—executive, legislative, or judicial—are busy people and, handled properly, are delighted to be relieved of the burdens of decision-making in complex matters. A Senator, for example, is usually much happier at a $1,000-a-plate fundraiser than trying to make sense out of Lebanon or Central America.

One evening in the fall of 1966, President Lyndon Johnson was prowling the Oval Office complaining that some writer had accused him of being the "dictator" of the Senate when he was Majority Leader. "Power," he said, "power, all they talk about is power. They think you buy it at the grocery store like sausages: 'just give me two pounds of power.' Sure I had power, but I couldn't shoot anybody no matter how much he deserved it. Sure, I ran the Senate, but do you know why?"

I allowed that I often wondered, and he grabbed me by the arm and said, "Because I did their work for them. A good third of them wouldn't roll over in bed for the Second Coming; they're bone lazy. So I did their work, they loved it, and behind my back they called me a 'dictator.'" The sermon ended with LBJ's version of the doctrine of Original Sin: "Johnny, just remember in this world no good deed goes unpunished."

The key to the power of the new class over the political class is its willingness to work, to prepare a briefing on El Salvador for "the Senator," to draft an opinion on a complex legal matter for a 75-year-old Supreme Court Justice,[159] to train the Cabinet Secretary for his budget hearings on the Hill. Moreover, the exponential growth of staffs over the past quarter of a century has led to "networking": as the mass has gotten critical, groups within it form sub-sets. The consequence is the emergence of "mandarinates" very much on the British and French models.

Admittedly, there have always been "old-boy" networks in American government, particularly in the military services. But nothing emerged that resembled the cohesive "Oxbridge" tradition in the British civil service that C. P. Snow illuminated in his novels, or the spider web of the French *Conseil d'état* which has its own West Point, the *Ecole Nationale d'Administration*, for the mandarins, suitably dubbed *Enarques*.[160]

---

[159]Some thirty years ago I suggested that legal scholars should explore the role of clerks in fashioning "their" judges' jurisprudence. I have lost the reference, but the thought was triggered by Supreme Court Justice Tom Clark's suddenly providing sharp, witty, and even serious opinions after a record of drabness perhaps equaled in my time only by Justice Owen Roberts. For a judicial year this comet rushed through the legal firmament and then Clark reverted to his earlier inertia. Unfortunately, when the study was done, it was an amateur hour—*The Brethren* by Bob Woodward and Scott Armstrong (New York: Simon and Schuster, 1980), consisting mainly of gossip about the Justices' interpersonal relations.

[160]The Mitterrand Government entered office vowing to reform this Platonic monstrosity, but the seriousness of its intentions can be gauged by the fact that those in charge of the revitalization are *Enarques*. To date some cosmetic changes in recruitment have been made, but the structure of the

Today in the United States the law schools seem to be the substitute for Oxford, Cambridge, and the *Ecole Nationale*. When you add to this the fact that at the time most "new class" staffers were in law school, lamentations about the repressive nature of American society had largely taken over the curricula from litigation, you get a clue to the source of the anti-American tropism. The cult of "public interest law" took the law schools by storm resulting in a large number of JDs scattered over a spectrum ranging from social workers to guerrillas, only a few of whom one would confidently hire to litigate a traffic case. They flocked into the newly enlarged federal social service agencies. (Most lawyers clearly follow traditional patterns, but the remainder is numerically quite substantial. Recall that with roughly 8 percent of the world's population, we have an estimated 80 percent of its lawyers.)

What this adds up to is the presence in the federal bureaucracy of a stratum of the new class, talented, hard-working, and linked together by membership in a political culture that is essentially anti-American, that sees "the Establishment" as reactionary and repressive, and automatically assumes an adversary position against tradition.

In 1978, for example, I was denounced to the rooftops for suggesting that in Iran the alternative to the Shah was a return to thirteenth century religious barbarism.[161] But internal structural aspects of Iranian society were irrelevant to my critics; to them it was enough that the United States had backed the Shah. The fate of the Iranian people at the hands of Islamic fanatics, who made the Shah's secret police look like the Salvation Army, was to them a matter of no concern. Again: narcissism.

To put it differently, this is a configuration with the courage of its convictions, but totally lacking in any concern about the consequences of its exploits. Those who in 1970 were holding monster rallies against our defense of the South Vietnamese, Laotians, and Khmer from Hanoi's totalitarian butchers, now have an epistemological "black hole": if you mention the Communist hecatomb in Indochina, they react as though

---

apparat has not been touched. Of course, as the Vichy episode demonstrated, a dedicated French civil servant will not be influenced by sentimental considerations.

[161]We had a number of Iranian students at The Fletcher School and Tufts University. They were bright, rich by comparison with their peers in Iran, and dedicated idealists, convinced the Shah was the incarnation of American-made evil. When I told them why the Jews of the Pale of Settlement in Russian-Poland always used to pray for the life of the Czar (because the next one was bound to be worse), they called me a cynical reactionary. Everyone *they* knew was for a liberal democracy. The only women they had ever seen in chadors were the servants who came in daily from the slums. Poor naive kids: I just hope they escaped the butchers. They deserve time to learn that in this life you deal with real options and, no matter how much you want it, you cannot create a third alternative with ideological rhetoric. A number of my onetime associates opposed the war in Vietnam because they believed there was a third alternative to American or Communist victory. They are still waiting, but very quietly.

they had never heard of the place. (Indeed, their passion abated almost overnight when President Nixon abolished the draft, fulfilling a prediction I made in 1967 which almost gave a "progressive" British journalist cardiac arrest.)[162]

Those ensconced in the bureaucracy have, of course, lines of communication to the private sector, particularly to a whole interlocking directorate of anti-Establishment research institutions clustered around the Washington-based Institute for Policy Studies. If, for example, a congressional aide needs a fast briefing paper for "the Congressman," on any topic from El Salvador to East Timor, or from the failings of the MX to the absurdity of building "star wars" ballistic missile defense systems, he can probably get one in half an hour from one or another brownstone on Capitol Hill. Needless to say, their common denominator is that strengthening American power is unnecessary and destabilizing.

As noted earlier in another context, the instant resource facilities of the new class have been imitated by others: two or three conservative research bodies such as the Heritage Foundation are on hand to provide material for those of their political persuasion. And the Committee on the Present Danger (of which I was a founder) unites John Kennedy-type liberals with internationalist conservatives in the effort to convince the political class that "making the world safe for diversity" (in JFK's phrase) is a precondition for making the United States safe for food stamps and welfare mothers.

However, the narcissists have seized the rhetorical heights. Their most potent thrust is apocalyptic: it is extremely difficult to counter rationally the charge that, say, by opposing a nuclear freeze, you joyfully anticipate turning the world into radioactive ashes. Viewed clinically, there is a weird paradox when a group of intellectuals are turned into banshees by the suggestion that since the Soviets have been experimenting with chemical weapons systems, we might be wise to explore the area. Indeed, if you showed them photographs of victims of Soviet biological and chemical warfare in Laos, Kampuchea, or Afghanistan you would doubtless be accused of faking the shots and the evidence, and of ignoring the fatal impact of bee-dung.

One of the most spectacular exercises in Corybantic chic is the annual festival of Hiroshima and Nagasaki. We are shown pictures of horribly burned women and children, protesters parade by candlelight, church bells toll. Those of us who were candidates for the invasion of the Japanese home islands can argue that the nuclear bombs were the catalyst

---

[162] Anthony Howard, who commented on my beastly cynicism in an article for *The Progressive*, in which he referred to me anonymously as a "high White House source" or some such.

that broke the Japanese will to resist (the March fire-bombing of Japanese cities killed more people than the two A-bombs without altering the Japanese army's fanaticism—see the American casualty figures for the invasion of Okinawa). We can further submit that it saved millions of Japanese from death by arms or starvation. Indeed, recently the man who was for twenty-five years President of the Japanese Medical Association, Dr. Taro Takemi, who in 1945 first diagnosed that the bombs were nuclear devices, argued that Japan was "saved" from starvation by the attacks. "The military," he said, "had driven Japan to a stage that if it could not win, it would not surrender." He was echoed by the eminent scholar and former U.S. Ambassador to Japan, Edwin O. Reischauer.[163]

However, I would not recommend making this argument without a substantial bodyguard to protect one from inflamed peace-lovers. "How can you engage in such callous, cost-benefit analysis," they will shriek, "when human lives are involved?" Besides, Dr. Takemi, as several Nobel laureates will doubtless assert, once diagnosed a case of amoebic dysentary as typhoid fever. Cost-benefit analysis is thus unhuman and inhumane, a technique no caring person would employ.

Double your bodyguard and ask, "I assume from your compelling respect for life that you are unconditionally opposed to the 1.3 million abortions that occur in the United States every year?"[164] Given the enormous overlap between the advocates of a nuclear freeze and the pro-abortion constituency, this puts the cat among the pigeons. Every argument for abortion except the preposterous one that a fetus is not a potential human being (no woman has ever given birth to a panda) is based on the most cold-blooded employment of cost-benefit analysis imaginable. But if you survive the encounter, you will discover that "freedom of choice" is "different."

A psychiatrist can look at this pathology abstractly, but in human terms it is extremely unpleasant to attend what has been billed as an intellectual exchange at a leading university and be treated as though you were

---

[163]"Japanese Doctor Says Bomb Averted Famine," an AP story carried on page 22, *New York Times*, August 6, 1983. Dr. Takemi added: "When one considers the possibility that the Japanese military would have sacrificed the entire nation if it were not for the atomic bomb attack, then this bomb might be described as having saved Japan." If you recall that at the meeting of the Supreme Imperial Council (the "Big Six") with the Emperor on the night of August 9, 1945 (East Longitudinal date) the vote was 3-3 for continuing the war and the Emperor broke the tie by calling for bearing the "unbearable" and capitulating, you get a sense of the fanaticism of the military. "Fat Boy" had hit Nagasaki shortly before they began their turbulent session. See John Toland, *The Rising Sun* (New York: Random House, 1970), pp. 810-814. (By West Longitudinal dating, these events occurred on August 8, 1945, in the United States.) Professor Reischauer's views, "Hiroshima bomb saved Japan from a worse fate," appeared in the *Boston Globe*, August 30, 1983.

[164]The latest official figure is 1,297,606 for 1980. There is no reason to believe it has dropped. (This, by the way, is three times the number of Americans killed in World War II.) Centers for Disease Control, Atlanta, Georgia, *Mortality, Morbidity Weekly Review*, Vol. 32, No. 255, February 11, 1983.

Heinrich Himmler at a meeting of Holocaust survivors. Speaking personally as one whose office was fire-bombed and family threatened for my support of the freedom of the South Vietnamese, I confess the events had a "chilling effect." I will tackle any opponent in a one-on-one radio or television format, but rarely subject myself to predictable attempted gang-rape by debating before an "intellectual audience."

All those factors—talent, messianic energy, intimidation, and, as Lyndon Johnson suggested, the laziness of those not driven by a vision of their natural ruling mission—have given the new class a role utterly disproportionate to its size. Moreover, while their whole sybaritic lifestyle rejects the Marxist-Leninist notion of a militarily organized cadre, they have absorbed the key lessons on the route to power: locate the fuse box and identify the crucial circuits.

Even a novice would know before arrival in Washington not to head for the Postal Service or Department of Agriculture. After a briefing by some old friends, he or she would for starters knock on the doors of the Corporation for Public Broadcasting, the Legal Services Corporation, the House Foreign Affairs or Intelligence committees, or any of the sub-agencies that pass out funds for legal aid, "community organization," or women and minorities. When you are plugged into the circuit, perhaps as a research aide to an Assistant Secretary of State, one day the phone will ring: a friend will call from the staff of a House subcommittee and say she has heard that Representative Chick Sales from Kensylvania has been put on the Foreign Affairs Committee, he thinks Evita still runs Argentina, and really wants to make a name for himself as a deep thinker. He needs a foreign affairs staffer and the word has been passed that you are the biggest thing since Henry Kissinger. (This brings a mutual chuckle—they both think Kissinger was a sinister force, but it does the job on Rep. Chick Sales.)

There then begins a modern version of Willi Münzenberg's "valet service." Some "resident fellow" at a new left think-tank writes a deep-think article in Sales' name which is sent to a leading journal in the area of foreign affairs which habitually accepts pieces "written by" Senators and Representatives. It is excerpted on the Op-Ed pages of several enlightened newspapers. "The Congressman" (a common style resembling the receptionist's "Doctor will see you now") is asked to address several conferences organized on planets in the new class solar system and is introduced to the luminaries whose names adorn the letterhead. In short, he is bagged: he needs the staffer more than she needs him.

She has invented his persona and taught him all the tricks that will keep the hard-line folks back in Kensylvania happy; how (to take a standard gambit) to vote for bills authorizing new weapons systems, but subsequently to oppose the necessary appropriations. She has, to summarize, capitalized on his egotism for the purposes of the new class. Willi Münzenberg, like Joe Hill, never died, or, if he did, was resurrected at Woodstock.

The time has come to leave the microcosm of innocents' clubs, milk cows, transmission belts, valet service, and useful idiots and shift to the macrocosm: the impact of Marxist-Leninist organizational theory on political developments at the national level throughout the world. Here we find the model of the cadre, or vanguard party, widely imitated (complete with the tactical techniques described above).

Passing over the obvious cases—nations such as those in Eastern Europe where Soviet hegemony is direct, or foreign Communist parties be they Trotskyist, Maoist, or even Albanian in persuasion—what we discover is that the Marxist-Leninist paradigm has been utilized by organizations with no allegiance to the doctrines of Marx and his disciples. In the same fashion that papal organization inspired ambitious monarchs in medieval Europe, Chiang Kai-shek built his Kuomintang (aided by Soviet advisers) with a Leninist blueprint.[165] Old wine, Chinese nationalism, was poured into the new, hopefully shatterproof, bottle.

All sorts of doctrinal elixirs have been similarly bottled, not the least of which was Adolf Hitler's "national socialism," which came complete with a Stalinist-type purge, the "night of the long knives" on June 30, 1934, in which what Stalin would have called "anti-party elements" were disposed of for allegedly conspiring against the Führer. The Nazi variety of the vanguard party, of course, spawned numerous offspring, notably in Austria and the Balkans, dedicated to the poisonous mixture of flaming nationalism and anti-Semitism. (Some might include Mussolini's *Fascisti*, which antedated Nazism by a decade, in the Leninist category, but *il Duce* was a one-man band who ignored the Fascist Grand Council until July 25, 1943, when it emerged from a coma and deposed him.)

It was in the colonial areas seeking independence that the vanguard concept really flourished. (There were even traces of it in Palestine among the eternally squabbling Zionist grouplets, particularly those of left-wing socialist ancestry which substituted Jewish nationalism for Marxism—or tried in truly Talmudic fashion to reconcile the two.[166]) In French Indo-

[165]A fascinating account is found in Harold R. Issacs, *The Tragedy of the Chinese Revolution* (Stanford: Stanford University Press, 1951). Issacs, who was a Trotskyist at the time (1938) the first edition of this work appeared (with an introduction by Leon Trotsky, which was unfortunately omitted from the Stanford edition), analyzed the Chinese political scene with the total impartiality of one who hoped both Chiang and the Stalinists would lose.

[166]The two main groups were Achdut HaAvoda and the more Marxist oriented HaAhomer HaAzair which in 1948 merged to form Mapam. Mapam had a pro-Soviet posture, but ironically almost at the moment of its creation it was sandbagged by the blatantly anti-Semitic purges in Soviet-dominated Eastern Europe which accompanied the Zhdanovshchina.

china, for example, in addition to Ho Chi Minh's Indochinese Communist Party, there were two nationalist groups (the VNQDD and Dai Viet) which drew their organizational inspiration from the Chinese Kuomintang.[167]

It would be boring to launch on a taxonomic travelogue. The point is that, whatever the substantive goals may be, the technique for achieving them is the same: all power in the hands of a militarily organized, highly disciplined elite purportedly endowed by history, race, ethnicity, or religion with doctrinal infallibility. It is a close question whether Ayatollah Khomeini would have shot Lenin before Vladimir Ilyich shot him, but they would both fire for the same principle. And if you examine the charge that Zimbabwe President Robert Mugabe has thrown against his old comrade-in-arms against the British, Joshua Nkomo, it comes down to the old Bolshevik dictum, "You can't be right against the Party."

Perhaps the perfect note on which to end this essay was sounded by Arthur Koestler in *Darkness at Noon*. Rubashov, the fallen Commissar patterned on Nicolai Bukharin, has been permitted to go for a walk in the prison exercise yard and is paired with "No. 406," whom he thinks of as "Rip Van Winkle": the old man has been imprisoned for about twenty years and seems slightly mad. "406" takes Rubashov's notebook and quickly draws a map of the USSR which he returns quietly humming a stanza of "The International." Later, when "406" tells Rubashov, pointing at the map, "one day we'll get there," the ex-Commissar realizes that the old man is convinced he is in a fascist jail![168]

That was a fictional vignette from the 1930s. Let us close with the May 1983 issue of the Soviet journal *Agitator of the Army and Navy* for a contemporary parallel.

Acting in an organized way and purposefully, the Jewish bourgeoisie seized key positions in the U.S. and continues to father into its hand ever greater spheres of influence. The leading banks, the largest financial establishments of the country either are the direct property of Jews-financiers,[169] or subordinate to their manifold influence. . . . Ninety-five percent of the largest military-industrial monopolies not only in the U.S. but in general in the countries of the West belong to the Jewish bourgeoisie and capital linked to it.

Joseph Goebbels may be dead but, as any *capo* will confirm, all Mafia "families" worship the same household gods.

---

[167]See I. Milton Sacks, "Marxism in Viet Nam," in Trager, editor, *op. cit.*, pp. 102-170.

[168]Arthur Koestler, *Darkness At Noon* (New York: Macmillan, 1941), pp. 128-133.

[169]For the benefit of skeptics, let me note that the word used in this article was Jew (*evrei*) not Zionist. The eternally hopeful may, however, console themselves that the vulgar *zhid* was not employed.

INSTITUTE FOR FOREIGN POLICY ANALYSIS, INC.
List of Publications

Foreign Policy Reports

DEFENSE TECHNOLOGY AND THE ATLANTIC ALLIANCE: COMPETITION OR COLLABORATION? By Frank T. J. Bray and Michael Moodie. April 1977. 42pp. $5.00.

IRAN'S QUEST FOR SECURITY: U.S. ARMS TRANSFERS AND THE NUCLEAR OPTION. By Alvin J. Cottrell and James E. Dougherty. May 1977. 59pp. $5.00.

ETHIOPIA, THE HORN OF AFRICA, AND U.S. POLICY. By John H. Spencer. September 1977. 69pp. $5.00. (Out of print).

BEYOND THE ARAB-ISRAELI SETTLEMENT: NEW DIRECTIONS FOR U.S. POLICY IN THE MIDDLE EAST. By R. K. Ramazani. September 1977. 69pp. $5.00.

SPAIN, THE MONARCHY AND THE ATLANTIC COMMUNITY. By David C. Jordan. June 1979. 55pp. $5.00.

U.S. STRATEGY AT THE CROSSROADS: TWO VIEWS. By Robert J. Hanks and Jeffrey Record. July 1982. 69pp. $7.50.

THE U.S. MILITARY PRESENCE IN THE MIDDLE EAST: PROBLEMS AND PROSPECTS. By Robert J. Hanks. December 1982. vii, 77pp. $7.50.

SOUTHERN AFRICA AND WESTERN SECURITY. By Robert J. Hanks. August 1983. 71pp. $7.50.

THE WEST GERMAN PEACE MOVEMENT AND THE NATIONAL QUESTION. By Kim R. Holmes. March 1984. 73pp. $7.50.

Special Reports

The papers in this series of Special Reports on Foreign Policy and National Security are addressed to current and emerging issues of critical importance and published on a "quick-reaction" basis. This series contains sufficient scope for treatment of all major issue areas of U.S. foreign policy and world affairs.

THE CRUISE MISSILE: BARGAINING CHIP OR DEFENSE BARGAIN? By Robert L. Pfaltzgraff, Jr., and Jacquelyn K. Davis. January 1977. x, 53pp. $3.00.

EUROCOMMUNISM AND THE ATLANTIC ALLIANCE. By James E. Dougherty and Diane K. Pfaltzgraff. January 1977. xiv, 66pp. $3.00.

THE NEUTRON BOMB: POLITICAL, TECHNICAL AND MILITARY ISSUES. By S. T. Cohen. November 1978. xii, 95pp. $6.50.

SALT II AND U.S. STRATEGIC FORCES. By Jacquelyn K. Davis, Patrick J. Friel and Robert L. Pfaltzgraff, Jr. June 1979. xii, 51pp. $5.00.

THE EMERGING STRATEGIC ENVIRONMENT: IMPLICATIONS FOR BALLISTIC MISSILE DEFENSE. By Leon Gouré, William G. Hyland and Colin S. Gray. December 1979. xi, 75pp. $6.50.

THE SOVIET UNION AND BALLISTIC MISSILE DEFENSE. By Jacquelyn K. Davis, Uri Ra'anan, Robert L. Pfaltzgraff, Jr., Michael J. Deane and John M. Collins. March 1980. xi, 71pp. $6.50 (Out of print).

ENERGY ISSUES AND ALLIANCE RELATIONSHIPS: THE UNITED STATES, WESTERN EUROPE AND JAPAN. By Robert L. Pfaltzgraff, Jr. April 1980. xii, 71pp. $6.50.

U.S. STRATEGIC-NUCLEAR POLICY AND BALLISTIC MISSILE DEFENSE: THE 1980S AND BEYOND. By William Schneider, Jr., Donald G. Brennan, William A. Davis, Jr., and Hans Rühle. April 1980. xii, 61pp. $6.50.

THE UNNOTICED CHALLENGE: SOVIET MARITIME STRATEGY AND THE GLOBAL CHOKE POINTS. By Robert J. Hanks. August 1980. xi, 66pp. $6.50.

FORCE REDUCTIONS IN EUROPE: STARTING OVER. By Jeffrey Record. October 1980. xi, 92 pp. $6.50.

SALT II AND AMERICAN SECURITY. By Gordon J. Humphrey, William R. Van Cleave, Jeffrey Record, William H. Kincade, and Richard Perle. October 1980. xvi, 65pp.

THE FUTURE OF U.S. LAND-BASED STRATEGIC FORCES. By Jake Garn, J. I. Coffey, Lord Chalfont, and Ellery B. Block. December 1980. xvi, 80 pp.

THE CAPE ROUTE: IMPERILED WESTERN LIFELINE. By Robert J. Hanks. February 1981. xi, 80pp. $6.50 (Hardcover, $10.00).

THE RAPID DEPLOYMENT FORCE AND U.S. MILITARY INTERVENTION IN THE PERSIAN GULF. By Jeffrey Record. February 1981. viii, 82 pp. $7.50 (Hardcover, $12.00).

POWER PROJECTION AND THE LONG-RANGE COMBAT AIRCRAFT: MISSIONS, CAPABILITIES, AND ALTERNATIVE DESIGNS. By Jacquelyn K. Davis and Robert L. Pfaltzgraff, Jr. June 1981. ix, 37pp. $6.50.

THE PACIFIC FAR EAST: ENDANGERED AMERICAN STRATEGIC POSITION. By Robert J. Hanks. October 1981. ix, 75pp. $7.50.

NATO'S THEATER NUCLEAR FORCE MODERNIZATION PROGRAM: THE REAL ISSUES. By Jeffrey Record. November 1981. vii, 102pp. $7.50.

THE CHEMISTRY OF DEFEAT: ASYMMETRIES IN U.S. AND SOVIET CHEMICAL WARFARE POSTURES. By Amoretta M. Hoeber. December 1981. xiii, 91pp. $6.50.

THE HORN OF AFRICA: A MAP OF POLITICAL-STRATEGIC CONFLICT. By James E. Dougherty. April 1982. xv, 74pp. $7.50.

THE WEST, JAPAN AND CAPE ROUTE IMPORTS: THE OIL AND NON-FUEL MINERAL TRADES. By Charles Perry. June 1982. xiv, 88pp. $7.50.

THE GREENS OF WEST GERMANY: ORIGINS, STRATEGIES, AND TRANSATLANTIC IMPLICATIONS. By Robert L. Pfaltzgraff, Jr., Kim R. Holmes, Clay Clemens, and Werner Kaltefleiter. August 1983. xi, 105pp. $7.50.

THE ATLANTIC ALLIANCE AND U.S. GLOBAL STRATEGY. By Jacquelyn K. Davis and Robert L. Pfaltzgraff, Jr. September 1983. viii, 44pp. $7.50.

WORLD ENERGY SUPPLY AND INTERNATIONAL SECURITY. By Herman Franssen, John P. Hardt, Jacquelyn K. Davis, Robert J. Hanks, Charles Perry, Robert L. Pfaltzgraff, Jr., and Jeffrey Record. October 1983. xiv, 93pp. $7.50.

Books

ATLANTIC COMMUNITY IN CRISIS: A REDEFINITION OF THE ATLANTIC RELATIONSHIP. Edited by Walter F. Hahn and Robert L. Pfaltzgraff, Jr. Pergamon Press, 1979. 386pp. $43.00.

SOVIET MILITARY STRATEGY IN EUROPE. By Joseph D. Douglass, Jr. Pergamon Press, 1980. 252pp. $33.00.

THE WARSAW PACT: ARMS, DOCTRINE, AND STRATEGY. By William J. Lewis. New York: McGraw-Hill Publishing Co., 1982. 471pp. $29.95.

Conference Reports

NATO AND ITS FUTURE: A GERMAN-AMERICAN ROUNDTABLE. Summary of a Dialogue. 1978. 22pp. $1.00.

SECOND GERMAN-AMERICAN ROUNDTABLE ON NATO: THE THEATER-NUCLEAR BALANCE. A Conference Report. 1978. 32pp. $1.00.

THE SOVIET UNION AND BALLISTIC MISSILE DEFENSE. A Conference Report. 1978. 26pp. $1.00.

U.S. STRATEGIC-NUCLEAR POLICY AND BALLISTIC MISSILE DEFENSE: THE 1980S AND BEYOND. A Conference Report. 1979. 30pp. $1.00.

SALT II AND AMERICAN SECURITY. A Conference Report. 1979. 39pp.

THE FUTURE OF U.S. LAND-BASED STRATEGIC FORCES. A Conference Report. 1979. 32pp.

THE FUTURE OF NUCLEAR POWER. A Conference Report. 1980. 48pp. $1.00.

THIRD GERMAN-AMERICAN ROUNDTABLE ON NATO: MUTUAL AND BALANCED FORCE REDUCTIONS IN EUROPE. A Conference Report. 1980. 27pp. $1.00.

FOURTH GERMAN-AMERICAN ROUNDTABLE ON NATO: NATO MODERNIZATION AND EUROPEAN SECURITY. A Conference Report. 1981. 15pp. $1.00.

SECOND ANGLO-AMERICAN SYMPOSIUM ON DETERRENCE AND EUROPEAN SECURITY. A Conference Report. 1981. 25pp. $1.00.

THE U.S. DEFENSE MOBILIZATION INFRASTRUCTURE: PROBLEMS AND PRIORITIES. A Conference Report (The Tenth Annual Conference, sponsored by the International Security Studies Program, The Fletcher School of Law and Diplomacy, Tufts University). 1981. 25pp. $1.00.

U.S. STRATEGIC DOCTRINE FOR THE 1980S. A Conference Report. 1982. 14 pp.

FRENCH-AMERICAN SYMPOSIUM ON STRATEGY, DETERRENCE AND EUROPEAN SECURITY. A Conference Report. 1982. 14pp. $1.00.

FIFTH GERMAN-AMERICAN ROUNDTABLE ON NATO: THE CHANGING CONTEXT OF THE EUROPEAN SECURITY DEBATE. Summary of a Transatlantic Dialogue. A Conference Report. 1982. 22pp. $1.00.

ENERGY SECURITY AND THE FUTURE OF NUCLEAR POWER. A Conference Report. 1982. 39pp. $2.50.

INTERNATIONAL SECURITY DIMENSIONS OF SPACE. A Conference Report (The Eleventh Annual Conference, sponsored by the International Security Studies Program, The Fletcher School of Law and Diplomacy, Tufts University). 1982. 24pp. $2.50.

PORTUGAL, SPAIN AND TRANSATLANTIC RELATIONS. Summary of a Transatlantic Dialogue. A Conference Report. 1983. 18pp. $2.50.

JAPANESE-AMERICAN SYMPOSIUM ON REDUCING STRATEGIC MINERALS VULNERABILITIES: CURRENT PLANS, PRIORITIES AND POSSIBILITIES FOR COOPERATION. A Conference Report. 1983. 31pp. $2.50.

NATIONAL SECURITY POLICY: THE DECISION-MAKING PROCESS. A Conference Report (The Twelfth Annual Conference, sponsored by the International Security Studies Program, The Fletcher School of Law and Diplomacy, Tufts University). 1983. 28pp. $2.50.

THE SECURITY OF THE ATLANTIC, IBERIAN AND NORTH AFRICAN REGIONS. Summary of a Transatlantic Dialogue. A Conference Report. 1983. 25pp. $2.50.